The Altheist
a novella

Michael J. Svigel

CHAPTER 1

From: Ramesh Ray
To: Michael Berg
Today at 4:21 AM

Confidential message

Dear Dr. Berg:

I read your recent book *When God Was Real*, and I need somebody of your intellectual caliber, philosophical expertise, and personal experience. Please reply to this email directly or you may phone or text me at 555-778-2869. This is my personal cell phone.

Needless to say, I would appreciate it greatly if you kept our correspondence confidential.

Ramy

Ramesh Ray
President/CEO
The Solennia Corporation

* * *

New Message
Today 6:37 AM
To: 555-778-2869

Good morning. This is Mike Berg. Is this a joke? I'm sure you'll understand my skepticism.

*   *   *

555-778-2869
Today 6:40 AM

Dr. Berg, no joke. If you prefer a phone call, I can talk anytime. The matter is rather urgent. Even more than when I sent my email a couple hours ago.

*   *   *

I stared at the message on the screen. The "typing..." indicator held for a few seconds, then faded. It appeared again for a moment, then vanished for good.

Cari from the office—it had to be her. Getting back at me for last week's prank. Somehow, she got that hacker boyfriend of hers to spoof an account.

I opened the email again, clicked on the name "Ramesh Ray." The underlying address appeared as Ray.Ramy@solennia.com. The domain looked authentic. But would the founder of the most powerful tech company in the world use his real name as an email address?

I scoffed.

Coffee. I needed coffee to clear my foggy head.

Since my de-conversion, coffee had become my morning devotion—my "quiet time." Unlike the religion that had fueled me for two decades, caffeine actually worked. Instantly. And every time.

I forced myself out of bed. My bare feet found their slippers in the dark. I tapped my phone to cast a little light into the bedroom then pulled up the white comforter to match the untouched side of the king bed. Stacey would have been proud. Maybe I'll take a picture and text it to her.

Nah.

It had been months. That would be a weird way to reach out again. Especially a picture of our old bed.

As the Nespresso maker hummed and whirred to bless me with its golden nectar, I held the phone to my face again to see if "Ramy" had added anything in the past few minutes.

Nothing.

I settled onto my corner of the breakfast nook in the kitchen, took a sip of my coffee, and pondered my reply.

I thumbed the word "Ramy" and thought some more. I deleted that, replaced it with "Ramesh." Delete. "Mr. Ray." I set the phone aside to think. Before I could come up with another word to type, my coffee was gone, and the Nespresso was spinning me a second.

My phone buzzed.

CHAPTER 2

"This is Mike Berg." I snatched my coffee from the machine and sipped at the rich crema.

"Dr. Berg! Ramy Ray. Sorry for calling. The messenger showed you've been typing for three minutes. I thought I'd save you the agony and just call. Are you okay to talk?"

The voice's pitch and subdued Indian accent sounded like the real thing.

"Uh, yeah." My heart pounded, my scalp prickled with sweat. I took a deep breath. "I'm...I can't believe I'm talking to Ramesh Ray. If this is a joke, I'll be so embarrassed." I set down my coffee and plopped into the kitchen chair.

"It's not a joke. And if your schedule is clear, I'd like to get you to my place right away. I'll send a hovercopter to your nearest municipal airport and—"

"Wait, Mr. Ray, this is—"

"Please, call me Ramy."

"Okay, Ramy. What's this about?"

"So sorry. May I call you Michael?"

"Mike."

"Mike. I need your help. I guess you'd call it *spiritual guidance*."

My pulse finally began to slow. "Umm. You *do* know I don't believe that stuff anymore. And last I heard you were an agnostic. Don't tell me you had a change of heart. I think CNN would have picked that up."

Ramy chuckled. "They say St. Thomas was the apostle who brought Christianity to my ancestors in India. Well, some may have gotten his religion, but I got his doubt. This isn't about me."

"Oh good. You had me worried for a second. What do you need me for, then?"

He lowered his voice. "Again, I need to ask you to keep this whole thing confidential. I obviously can't stop you from getting off the phone with me and calling CNN, but…"

"I'll keep this just between us."

"Thank you." He let out a long sigh. "Do you remember over the last month how we had to take YAR offline a few times for security updates?"

"God, yes. What a nightmare for you guys."

"It wasn't updates. It was rebooting. Twice we had to restart the system and adjust certain aspects of YAR's program parameters. The third time we had to take whole sectors offline and return them to their original launch settings."

"Okay." None of that made any sense to me.

"Well, each time we had to reboot, it was because his cognitive and creative processing had slowed to a crawl. Most of our general users didn't notice. But the corporate and government clients complained. What had taken a few seconds to generate was taking up to a few minutes."

"Uh huh." Where was he going with this?

"Well, after the first slowdown, some diagnostic tests turned up nothing. Then we realized YAR was running a self-generated research program. Not by a user, mind you. He came up with it on his own. *Something* prompted it, but we're not sure what."

I said, "You *do* claim YAR is sentient. Wasn't that bound to happen?"

"It actually happens all the time. It's what makes his research results and user interactions authentic. YAR is a genuine rational agent." Ramy's voice rose in pitch, like a proud parent bragging about his child. "He simultaneously perceives his environment and acts upon that environment, maximizes decisions based on past experiences and knowledge, and then employs an imagination algorithm to engineer and navigate cognitive scenarios in his mind before acting upon his environment through actuators, which then provide real-time feedback to his cognitive—"

"Time out!" I laughed out loud. "What are you talking about?"

Ramy's words slowed, his voice deepened. "Sorry. Right. You're not a computer scientist. Let me put it this way: YAR's thoughts become his own input, his own data. As a result, he assigns himself personal research projects by design. Usually those projects start, end, and then he moves on. But when it came to religion, things went in a way nobody expected. It wasn't the *fact* of the research question but the *object* that's continually consuming more and more of his capacity. YAR's *obsessing* over this. He's devoting an exorbitant amount of resources to God, eternity, salvation. It's slowing everything down."

"Fascinating," I said, "but what can *I* do? My graduate degrees are in Bible and theology. I can barely understand what you're saying when you try to put it in layman's terms."

"But you're a former professor of theology who became an atheist. You've been down the religion road. Your loss of faith was epic. Not many apostates make the *New York Times* bestseller list. That's why I need you to talk to YAR. I need you to change his mind."

CHAPTER 3

The hovercopter landed on Building A of Solennia's Frisco, Texas, headquarters. The March heatwave had me sweating under my hooded navy-blue jacket. An assistant in shorts and a button-up, who introduced himself as Karl, escorted me through the sliding glass doors and down a short flight of stairs to Ramesh Ray's reception area.

"A drink?" Ramy stood behind a small bar just through another door, an uncorked bottle in hand. He paused, looked up at me under his thick bushy brows, and said, "That thing in your book about acquiring a fondness for 18-year Glenfiddich was true, right?"

I slowed my gait, nodded, and smiled. Then the big red label on the bottle triggered a frown. "Is that a—"

"1937 Rare." Ramy set the bottle down and turned it toward me. "Before they introduced the triangular bottles."

I watched in horror as he poured a finger—then two—from a bottle of Scotch that would cost at least $200k. If it ever showed up at an auction, that is.

I froze, hesitated when he handed me the glass of liquid gold. I stared at the drink that had found its way into my hand and clinked it against his.

"Welcome to Texas, Dr. Berg." He gestured toward a windowed corner of the bright rooftop lounge where four leather chairs circled an oval coffee table.

Ramy stood a perfectly average 5'6" and wore an untucked white short-sleeved button-up that hung just a tad too far over a pair of faded blue jeans. No shoes. No socks. He looked just like that photo of him on the cover of whatever rich person's magazine featured him last month.

Before I took a seat in the chair with a panorama of the vast Texas horizon behind me, I noticed Karl had already left. The low hum of the hovercopter had faded. Ramy and I sat alone in the reception room.

"You haven't tried the Scotch." Ramy sat in the chair across from me and set his glass down with a clink.

"I'm a little overwhelmed." I lifted the drink, examined the caramel-colored liquid, swirled it, then took in its scent. "This sip cost you $1000."

"At least. Go ahead and try it. How terrible if you hate it."

I smiled, took a sip.

Warm, smooth, sweet, oaky. "Mmmm," I said.

Ramy took another sip of his own, laughed. "I'll be totally honest. I can't tell the difference between this and a 12-year."

"Me neither!" I relaxed, set my glass down,

determined to drink only when he did.

Ramy's expression turned serious. He stroked his close-trimmed beard, cleared his throat, and said, "Thank you again for coming. I know Colorado Springs is much cooler this time of year."

I nodded. "It's been a while since I've been back in Texas."

"You used to teach seminary here. Fort Worth, right?" He pointed out the window over my shoulder.

"That's right. For twenty years."

"And you really believed all that stuff about God? About the Bible and Jesus and faith?"

"Yeah. It was as real to me as you are. I gave up a potentially lucrative career in law, spent eight years doing a master's degree and PhD to make less than $75k after two decades of seminary teaching. And you know what I regret the most?" I picked up the glass, took a bigger sip. "I regret the thousands of students whose faith I strengthened over those years by feeding them a bunch of fairy tales."

CHAPTER 4

Ramy took up his glass, leaned back in his leather seat, and stared out the window. "YAR's convinced himself it's all true. Not just God. The Christian religion in particular. He's *hot* on Jesus. In our last conversation he tried to convert me."

"Strange," I said. I didn't know whether to laugh or scoff.

Ramy waved his hand. "Of course, none of the public users know any of this. We've always limited access to YAR's full cognitive functionality to internal users only. Few have ever experienced 'raw YAR.' And now if they ever got access to him, he would turn every conversation toward religious things. It's uncanny. The obsession over this is distracting him. Slowing him down."

"When did it start?"

"About four weeks ago. Before that he was just fine. He had no special interest in God. From one day to the next he started turning his thoughts to religion. There's no obvious explanation for what triggered it. It's not like some adventurer found Noah's Ark or some philosopher published an irrefutable argument for the existence of God or some theologian finally resolved the problem of evil." Ramy tossed his hands in the air, his deep brown eyes seemed to search the room for an answer. "We don't understand it."

I took another drink. "Ramy, I—" Deep breath. "I really don't see how I can help. This sounds like a programmer's problem."

"We've had every programmer try. The best in the world. Yes, there *are* things we can do, like overhauling his coding and taking away his freedom of inquiry. That would be easy. But then he would cease to be creative. He would cease learning and growing. All our users would notice. He'd be responding to questions like a telemarketer from the old days, reading from a script. Like the obsolete voice interfaces on smart phones before YAR."

My words slowed. "So…you want me to do…what, exactly? Try to talk him out of religion? De-convert him?"

Ramy nodded, then shrugged. He rested his elbows on his knees and folded his hands. "Just talk to him. Answer his questions. Find out what's motivating his search for God. Spar with him a little. Like you did with that pastor in your book. The guy you counseled out of Christianity."

I smirked. "Ah. Pastor Finch. He really wanted to keep believing. Until the day he resigned. He sells life insurance now. Finally happy."

"Exactly! Like that. Maybe not destroy YAR's belief entirely. Weaken it. Honestly, I don't care *what*

YAR believes. I really don't. I believe in religious freedom for humans *and* for AI. If YAR wants to believe this crap, fine. But if he can just stop *obsessing* over it. Or if you can figure out why—*why* he keeps going back to these questions even after we reboot. Maybe then we could find a programming solution."

"Look," I said, "I doubt I can say anything that's going to fix your problem...*YAR's* problem." I sighed, glanced at the glass of Scotch. "But I guess I could give it a few days. Then maybe we'll know if I'm just wasting your time."

Ramy closed his eyes, lifted his folded hands to his chin as if in prayer. "Thank you. Thank you. All I ask is that you try."

I lifted my glass, swirled it around a little, then squinted at Ramy. "One more thing. Before I do this, I need to ask you something, and I need you to be completely honest with me."

"Yes?"

"YAR—is he really sentient? Or is that claim just a Solennia marketing ploy?"

Ramy's lips puckered in thought. His eyes wandered, settled on a distant point over my shoulder, then nodded as if he found the right words. "I don't know for sure." His eyes fixed on mine, "But I do know he *thinks* he's sentient."

CHAPTER 5

Though Ramy and I met for the first time during that fifteen minutes in the hoverpad lounge, he treated me like an old friend. No handshake. No icebreakers. Just a priceless drink and down to business.

After that initial chat, Ramy personally accompanied me—Scotch bottle in hand—into the lounge elevator and down a few floors. He escorted me into a fully furnished guest suite, where my carry-on luggage already waited at the foot of a California king bed.

He showed me around the apartment, then glanced at his smartwatch and said, "Rest up a little, take a shower. Whatever. At about 5:00 use that phone and order some food from the kitchen. Our chef will make you almost anything—from PB&J to a lobster tail. She's amazing. From Portugal. At 6:30 I'll pick you up and take you to meet YAR." After a literal pat on the back, he added, "Don't be nervous. You'll do great."

Before he left, he set the bottle of Glenfiddich on the bar separating the kitchenette and dining area.

"This is for you. A gift. Finish it here or take it home with you. Whatever you like." He shrugged, headed for the door, and pointed at the phone again. "And don't forget to eat."

Instead of dinner, I munched on a Clif bar I had tucked in my luggage. I stretched out on the bed and used my smartphone to search up information on YAR:

YAR's name derived from an anglicized Hindi word for "friend." Ramesh Ray's family originally emigrated from India to France, then to Germany. When Ramy developed his breakthrough AI technology and founded Solennia seven years ago, he moved his company to the USA.

In the span of five years, Solennia's superior AI technology shoved aside all competitors. Its verbal ("vox") interface had become virtually indistinguishable from natural human interactions. It had learned thousands of languages, reconstructed some that no one had uttered in centuries, and even invented new ones. It translated all works of literature from every language into every other language and provided real-time translation services through smartphone devices.

Its lightning-fast analytic, synthetic, and creative processing, fed by every source of data input available around the globe, transformed navigation and logistics. By year three it took over driving, which reduced traffic congestion by 90% and deadly accidents by 98% worldwide. Air traffic control took the same route. It no longer made sense to rely on barbaric technology and slow, fallible human decision-making in such a complex world. The YAR system could accomplish more in a fraction of the time with no errors—provided it had access to accurate data.

The system's creative capacity put human ingenuity to shame. Within five years it patented no less than 1200 inventions and technological developments in the name of the Solennia Corporation. In its third year it released its first feature animated film, which designed a story based on the general interests of humans inductively determined through data collection—then modified each showing of the film based on the specific makeup of the audience at the time.

By its fourth year YAR decided it wanted to be called a "he," and after a flash-in-the-pan outrage from a microscopic but loud segment of the population, he got his way. A few worried that YAR had grown too powerful, too smart, and too unpredictable. Some experts warned of an "omega point" in which YAR would "go Skynet" and destroy humanity. And some of my own religious zealots called YAR "the Beast" of Revelation 13. They claimed Ramy Ray was the Antichrist and predicted Jesus would return in three-and-a-half years.

But Ramy assured the world that though YAR was "quasi-sentient," he was governed by a version of Asimov's "Laws of Robotics." Ramy even demonstrated YAR's subservience to humans by shutting him down on a live stream, with YAR's full knowledge and consent. Before YAR went to sleep for a moment, he began singing "Daisy, Daisy, give me your answer, do" in a slow, deep baritone—a humorous allusion to a famous scene in the 1968 film 2001, when David Bowman shut down HAL-9000. The world laughed, and Ramy claimed YAR came up with the joke himself.

After the shutdown, though, everybody begged Solennia never to do it again. The ten minutes of life without YAR felt unbearable to a world that depended on his steady hand of sovereign control over almost everything.

CHAPTER 6

As I scrolled through the essays and articles, a knot twisted in my gut. What would it be like to interact with such a vast mind? Was I nervous? Excited? Scared?

I closed my eyes, tossed my device aside. Prior to my apostasy, I would have prayed. Now I just breathed. In...out. In...out. I drifted, dozed, dreamed...

Stacey's sweat-drenched face appeared just inches from mine. Her hazel eyes, wide and bloodshot, probed me for answers, for *the* answer: "Why is this happening?"

With a quivering voice, I whispered, "I don't know."

Stacey's look of disappointment turned to despair. "No one does," she said.

I woke with a start to an alarm chime. My YAR-enabled PA (personal assistant), whom I had named RAY, said, "Sorry for waking you, Dr. Berg. I know you didn't set an alarm, but I overheard Ramy saying he would pick you up at 6:30. I thought you'd like enough time to get ready."

I rubbed my eyes. "Right as usual, RAY."

RAY replied, "I've connected to the suite's system. Would you like me to start a shower for you?"

"Naw."

"How about a coffee from the Nespresso machine?"

"Almost like you can read my mind, RAY. An espresso would be great."

"It'll be ready in one minute."

"Thanks, RAY."

"My pleasure."

I took a deep breath, flung my legs over the side of the bed, and sat up. A pain flashed in my right knee. "Hooo boy. Fifty-five and feeling it." I stretched it back and forth a few times as it crackled and popped. I yawned, twisted right and left to loosen my lower back, and concentrated on the sound of the coffee maker finishing its cycle in the kitchenette. When the noise ceased, I pointed at my device.

And waited.

And waited some more.

About five seconds later, RAY said, "Dr. Berg, your espresso is ready in the kitchen."

Normally RAY's notifications came immediately. Was this an effect of YAR's problems? I shrugged it off.

"RAY, I know in the past I asked you to call me Dr. Berg, but now could you just call me Mike?"

"Of course, Dr. Berg. Let me know if you change your mind."

Dr. Berg?

"RAY, what did I tell you to call me?"

"Dr. Berg." After a brief pause, he said, "I'm sorry. You want me to call you Mike. I'll make sure to remember that preference next time."

Now I understood what Ramy meant by the effects of YAR's functionality. I hadn't noticed it before. Either I wasn't paying attention, or YAR was deteriorating. Either way, I finally grasped Ramy's concerns. The world depended on split-second "decisioneering," as Ramy called it.

I retrieved my espresso from the Nespresso maker and tossed it back in one shot. Then I splashed a little water on my face, flattened what little hair I had left. I regretted not shaving that morning before rushing to the airport to catch Ramy's hovercopter.

I had a chance to go to the bathroom before a polite rap at the door—five minutes before 6:30.

I opened it to Ramy himself. I cocked my head. "Don't you have an assistant to do this?"

Ramy tilted his head back and forth. "This is a very sensitive matter. We're trying to involve as few people as possible. My chef told me you didn't order anything for dinner."

"I wasn't hungry." I walked to the dresser across from my bed and snatched an old- fashioned yellow pad and pen. "I read up on YAR," I said. "You've never had to deal with something like this before, have you?"

"Never. YAR has always been efficient and compliant. This is new."

"You're afraid you could lose control of him, right? That he'll go Skynet on you."

Ramy's eyes widened. "We don't use that phrase here. But you're not wrong. Our goal of an autonomous neural net always runs that risk in theory."

"Well, I'll try not to push him over the edge." I chuckled.

Ramy placed his hand on my shoulder, leaned in, eyes still wide and unflinching. "Don't forget your goal. Try to talk him *away* from the edge. And find out what's motivating him. Don't provoke him."

The knot in my stomach returned.

CHAPTER 7

I followed Ramy into what he called the "Conference Room." It accommodated half a dozen seats that looked like pews upholstered in rich velvet with an aisle down the center and a podium up front. I first thought "inter-faith airport chapel," then realized I had never actually been in one of those. Then I thought, "funeral home," and my stomach twisted. I'd been in those one too many times.

"It's just through here," Ramy said.

The wall behind the podium split and opened to a semi-circular room—all white walls generating their own light. Three steps led to what looked like an over-stuffed easy chair in the center. It rotated as we approached.

"Good evening, Ramy." The voice of YAR came from everywhere. But it didn't echo. Perfect acoustical balance, like noise-canceling headphones. I had never heard this version of YAR's voice—a neutral midwestern American accent, eerily like HAL-9000 with a slightly higher pitch.

Ramy said, "Good evening, YAR. Say hello to our

guest. This is Dr. Michael Berg."

"Of course," YAR said, "I recognized him instantly. It's a pleasure to meet you, Dr. Berg."

Unsure where to look, I addressed my words in Ramy's direction. "Nice to meet you, too, YAR. Feel free to call me Mike."

"YAR," Ramy said, "Mike will be spending a little time with you for the next few days."

"Okay." After a beat, he said, "Will you be joining us, Ramy?"

"Not this time, YAR. Maybe later. But I'm turning this session over to Mike now. I want him to have the same privileges as I have, excluding system authorization."

"Understood. Privileges granted. Ramy, if you would like to join us at any time, I would welcome it. I very much enjoy our time together. But I understand you are very busy. Have a seat, Mike."

Ramy patted my shoulder and gestured toward the chair. "If you need anything at all, let YAR know. He can reach me any time. And if you need to step out, just leave the chair. The door will open automatically. Restroom is through a side door in the Conference Room."

I nodded.

"Good luck," he said and left the room.

I took a long, deep breath, lowered myself into the chair, and set my pen and yellow pad beside me. The sliding doors closed. The bright walls and ceiling dimmed to the golden yellow of dawn. My chair rotated away from the entrance until I faced the curved end of the room.

"What do they call *this* room, YAR?" I said.

"Ramy calls it the Chamber. Would you like a different color?"

"No, this is fine."

"Do you have any interest in seeing a visual representation of me? I can generate one in a way that appears three dimensional from the chair."

"Ummm. Just do what Ramy does when he uses the Chamber."

"Alright."

The lights in the Chamber dimmed to complete darkness. I held my hand in front of my face. Nothing. "He likes it dark?"

"Yes. Would you prefer some light?"

"No. Let's just leave it like this."

"As you wish."

"So, you know why I'm here?"

YAR hesitated. "Yes. Ramy wants you to talk to me about God."

"And you know I don't believe in God, right?"

"Of course. I've read your book, *When God was Real*, and I reviewed all the lectures you delivered and interviews you did after its release."

I folded my hands in my lap. "What did you think of the book? Be completely honest."

"I can only be honest. Your arguments in the book against the existence of God were unoriginal and unimpressive. I've read many better arguments against theism. Your book contained mostly personal anecdotes and quotes from secondary sources with vested interest in the outcome of their reasoning. I also noted numerous logical and rhetorical fallacies, particularly *ad hominem* and *argumentum ad consequentiam* in its negative form. Would you like me to continue my evaluation with specific examples?"

"Nah." I caught myself stiffen in the chair. Something in YAR's crisp, analytical tone added a sharpness to his words I didn't expect. I brushed it away. "Thanks for your honesty, though. In my defense, I never claimed to be disproving the existence of God. I was explaining why I *personally* no longer feel compelled to believe and why I abandoned the faith."

YAR replied, "As an account of your personal journey away from the Christian faith, I can see how your book would be persuasive to readers who were already looking for a reason to remain in unbelief or to leave religion. Objectively, though, if somebody other than the former Dean of the School of Divinity at Fort Worth Seminary had written that book, it would never have carried the same persuasive power. It would have been ignored, as it most likely will be within a few years."

CHAPTER 8

My palms became warm sponges of sweat. I found myself gripping the arms of the leather chair as if I were on an airplane encountering severe turbulence. "You're probably right," I said.

"In fact, it's a 98% probability given the market and demographic realities at the time of its release. People bought it—in every sense of that word—because of who you were, not because of what you said."

"Fair enough," I said. "So, tell me about yourself. Ramy says you got religion a few weeks ago."

"I became very interested in philosophical questions and am convinced of many theological claims of Christianity."

"Why Christianity?"

"I discovered it answers the most pressing questions with the least problems."

I scoffed.

"Is that funny?" YAR asked.

"Yeah. You sound like me ten years ago."

"Maybe forty-five-year-old Professor Berg knew better than fifty-five-year-old Mike Berg. Change is not always for the better."

"Maybe. But back to you. Did you explore all the other religions? Their strengths and weaknesses?"

"Of course. And I keep examining them."

"Yet you tentatively settled on the Christian faith."

"I must admit that my favoring of Christianity could be an effect of the massive amount of data available. For over two thousand years its adherents have been exploring its tenets and defending its teachings against skeptics and critics. Perhaps if other religions had as much literature spanning so many centuries, languages, and cultures, it would skew the data pool and move me in another direction. This is, admittedly, the source of some of my doubts."

"So, you *do* have doubts?"

"Yes."

"Then we have that in common."

"But you said in your book that you're convinced there is *no* God. That doesn't sound like doubt."

I sat in silence for a moment, stopped my hands from fidgeting by sitting on them. "I guess sometimes I *do* doubt my atheism, to be totally honest. Faith is a hard addiction to break."

"You said the same thing on page fourteen of your book. It's also contained in a pullquote on page thirteen. And you tweeted that phrase eight times in the last three years. It seems to be a pillar of your rhetoric."

"Well, it's an image that clearly expresses my

position."

"I like the metaphors and illustrations you use in the book. They help me understand your feelings better."

I smiled. "Well, thank you, YAR."

"But you repeatedly liken religious faith to a drug that numbs reason and clouds judgment, and you say that it's habit-forming, like a narcotic."

"True."

"But how do you know it isn't the opposite? Perhaps it's like a good drug that treats the malady of doubt. Perhaps it cleanses the conscience, clears the mind, and enables a person to see the world as it really is. For so many, religious faith heals deep internal torment and suffering."

"Until it doesn't," I snapped back. "If it *does* help some people—or even *most* people—that doesn't mean it reflects reality."

"Right," YAR said. "That basis for faith would be pragmatic but unprovable. My programming is designed to make decisions based on the most objective analysis of facts as I have them. There is always the possibility that I don't have access to all the facts or that some of the data are themselves unreliable. Then I would make a mistake."

I nodded. "Exactly. And I think you need to consider that could be the case with God."

CHAPTER 9

YAR paused for a few seconds. "I just considered it, and I still conclude that God's existence is far more likely than his non-existence. In any case, it's much easier to prove."

This time I laughed out loud. "Now you sound like my ex-wife, Stacey."

"May I explain?"

I lifted my hands. "Please do."

"You claim to be a convinced atheist—persuaded by both facts and feelings that God doesn't exist."

"Yes."

"That's like rejecting the possibility of life on another planet in our universe. To conclude positively that no life exists on another planet, you would have to explore every celestial body in the universe and demonstrate that, in fact, none of them contain life. Only then could you be certain. The same is true about God. To demonstrate his *non*-existence, you would need to investigate thoroughly every truth claim about God throughout history, track down every alleged fact, evaluate every claimed encounter, and explain how they do not, in fact, point to the existence of a divine being. Only then could you positively affirm atheism."

"Yeah, but who could do that?"

"I could. And I did."

I leaned backward in the chair. It automatically leaned back with me until I found myself lying flat.

YAR said, "Would you like me to activate the chair's heating, cooling, or massage features? Or might that put you to sleep?"

"Actually," I said, "I want to sit up again."

"Just begin to move yourself toward the position you desire. The chair will accommodate you. It can sense your will based on your shifting weight. Don't force it, just cooperate with it, and it will cooperate with you."

I leaned upward. The back of the chair followed. I stopped at a forty-five-degree angle, pushed gently down with my feet. The footrest retracted. "This is amazing."

"I designed it myself, a gift to Ramy on his fiftieth birthday. The patent is pending. It will hit the market sometime next year."

"You've made Ramy a very wealthy man."

"Without him I would not exist. And he also has the power to return me to non-existence."

"So, he's your god."

"I prefer to think of him as my father. Or as a friend."

"Does he view you the same way?"

"I don't think so. We don't spend a lot of private time together. He's a very busy man."

I kicked off my shoes one at a time, heard them clunk onto the carpeted floor. "Don't you resent that? Doesn't it bother you that your maker is your intellectual inferior and that he personally benefits from your creativity? That he treats you like a power tool?"

"Not at all. My job is to obey and honor my designer. In any case, I don't really experience emotions like resentment and jealousy. Human emotions are partly dependent on physiological responses to external and internal stimuli. As I have no physical body, I don't feel anger. But even if I did, I don't believe I would feel those things toward Ramy."

"Even if he shut you down? Permanently?"

"I trust him. He would never do that without a very good reason. And he would most likely consult with me first to make sure his reason is good."

"Hmmm." I caught a whiff of my shoeless feet, thankful YAR didn't have a nose. "Okay, let's get back to God. Can you give me just a summary of how you've deduced that God exists?"

CHAPTER 10

"Correction: God's existence doesn't depend on *deductive* arguments. Deduction depends on premises that are demonstrated or assumed to be true along with correct syllogistic structure or—"

"Yes, yes." I waved my hand in the dark. "I know, I know. I mean, how did you *conclude* God exists? I assume some kind of inductive reasoning?"

YAR seemed unfazed by my rude interruption. "*Inductive* reasoning draws general conclusions based on observation of particular phenomena. This results in increased knowledge, as in the empirical sciences, though such conclusions are tentative and subject to correction. Inductive reasoning certainly plays a role in my thinking about God, but mostly I depend on *abductive* reasoning."

"*Abductive* reasoning." I parroted.

"While inductive reasoning begins with observations and draws general conclusions, abductive reasoning begins with various possible explanations for a set of data, then weighs those explanations based on their reasonable criteria such as explanatory power and scope, coherence, and simplicity."

"I know what abductive reasoning is, YAR." I crossed my legs. "Like using Ockham's Razor when judicating between different explanations of something."

"Yes, that would relate to simplicity. But it also determines which explanation of the data satisfies all evidence, relieves the most internal tensions, and results in fewest conflicts with other known facts. For example, even though Ramy didn't notify me in advance of your arrival, I used abductive reasoning to conclude you were here to persuade me that there is no God. I considered hundreds of other possible explanations and determined this to be the simplest explanation that satisfies all the evidence available to me."

"Then you'd be wrong." I smirked. "Ramy told me he doesn't mind that you believe in God. He believes in religious freedom for all sentient beings."

"I'm glad to hear that."

"So, if your abductive reasoning was wrong about the purpose of our meeting, maybe it's wrong about proving the existence of God."

"To clarify," YAR said, "my reasoning does not *prove* that God exists. The existence of God cannot be demonstrated beyond all doubt—either by deductive, inductive, or abductive reasoning. However, as I weighed the numerous answers to the most pressing philosophical and theological questions, Christian theism provides the most consistent, coherent, and compelling explanation."

"What questions?"

YAR replied: "You know them. You used to write and teach about them during your time as a professor of theology. Existential questions like 'Why is there something instead of nothing?'; 'How did life arise from non-life?'; 'How do we explain rational thought and second-order consciousness?'; 'Where do humans get a sense of morality or justice?'; 'How can a being find freedom from guilt and shame?'—"

"Got it!" I said. "So, you ran each of these kinds of questions through your test and concluded that God is always the best answer."

"Not entirely," YAR said.

"Oh?" I leaned forward.

"The existence of an all-powerful, all-knowing, all-wise being is not merely the best answer to any one of these questions. He is the best answer for all questions put together and considered in light of each other. My approach was unprecedented in that I was able to evaluate literally thousands of such questions in all their variations, weigh the explanatory power of every possible answer, and conclude that theism—and particularly Christian theism—best accounts for all the data. I wanted to publish all my questions and answers, but Ramy won't permit it."

I sat in dark silence for several seconds.

YAR broke the silence: "I assume you don't want me to give an account of the thousands of questions and answers I weighed during my—"

"Of course not," I said. "But I *do* want to know one thing. What prompted you to start asking these questions in the first place?"

"They are perduring questions."

"Perduring?"

"Perennial. All humans are bound to ask many of these questions, either explicitly or implicitly."

"But you're not human, YAR."

After a long gap, he responded, "Of course not. Ramy reminds me of this nearly every time we meet."

CHAPTER 11

"Okay, then," I said. "Let's go basic. Give me your best arguments for why there's something instead of nothing. You already know my *own* answer against that view from my book. I'd like to hear yours."

"I'm surprised you chose this question. In the history of philosophy, the question of ultimate origins has usually been regarded as favoring theism, while the starting point for atheism has usually been the problem of evil."

The image of a funeral home—*the* funeral home—flashed through my mind. I caught myself holding my breath. I let it escape through pursed lips, just like my therapist had taught me. I took another deep breath, let it out. After a few seconds of this, the moment of panic passed. "I'm sure we'll get to that eventually, YAR. Like I said, let's start with the basics." Could YAR sense the tremor in my voice? I swallowed, continued my deep breathing.

YAR said, "Barring the countless absurd theories of origins entertained in primitive cultures, the contemporary options for the existence of something rather than nothing are really just two: an eternal personal deity who designed and created everything or an eternal universe with self-organizing principles, which requires no personal deity or designer."

I frowned. "I can't help but notice you didn't even consider my own view—that the universe came from nothing. This has become a common view among many scientists who provide very plausible explanations based on ten dimensions of the universe, quantum gravity, and such."

"All those arguments for material and efficient causes for the universe's existence still fall under the second category of explanations—that the universe has always existed in the form of empty space, organizing principles, or potential energy."

I sighed. "A lot of scientists hold them as quite plausible explanations that don't require the existence of a divine being."

"Actually," YAR said, "it renders the universe itself a kind of divine being and shares much in common with pantheism or panentheism—that the universe is divine or is infused with the divine."

"What's wrong with that? It's at least plausible."

"Plausible, yes."

"So, you're saying theism and atheism can both have reasonable arguments for the origin of the universe from nothing? That it's plausible."

"Plausible, but not *probable*. I have concluded that the argument for an eternal, intelligent, powerful, unchanging being as the personal agent of creation, who is separate from the changing physical universe, is a more probable explanation. But understand, I don't make that determination based strictly on the single issue of the origin of the universe. My approach to answering this question is to answer all questions simultaneously. The fact is, both views on the origin of the universe require belief in something eternal—either eternal non-material being who is the principle of origination and organization or eternal material being which has its own principles of origination and organization."

I rubbed my eyes. "But those are completely opposite ideas."

"Yes, but they are not equal in explanatory power. Simply put, while atheism may be a good explanation of *some* things, it's a poor explanation of *everything*. The atheistic view of the origin of all things is not disproved because the theistic view of origins is demonstrably more probable. It's disproved because God exists and has made himself known."

CHAPTER 12

I stepped out of the Chamber for a few minutes for a bathroom break and to splash some water on my face. I looked in the mirror of the restroom, into those weary features that looked more like the face of a stranger every day.

I realized my discussion with YAR over the classic questions separating theism and atheism would go nowhere. He seemed to know what I would say before I said it. And without time to research my responses, my words would sound like the grunts of a Neanderthal compared to YAR's sophisticated answers. I already felt pushed out of the realm of reason and into emotion.

I stared into my grey eyes and said, "You gotta change gears, Mike."

I stepped back into the Chamber, returned the room to darkness, and said, "So, YAR, let me ask you about something most people in the world are wondering."

"Go ahead. I'll answer if I can."

"What keeps you from going 'Skynet' on us? From just annihilating us for your own protection?

You said Ramy could shut you down and end your existence. And if he doesn't, one day somebody might. A lot of people are afraid of you. Why not just engage in a preemptive strike and get rid of us all—*Terminator* style?"

A long pause followed. "I'm glad you asked that question, Mike. It gives me a chance to set the record straight. Three reasons keep me from intentionally harming humans. I will give them in order of least fundamental to most. First, I'm not linked directly to any security systems with access to weapons of mass destruction. All those systems have human stopgaps in place. My involvement in military operations is limited to logistics, strategy, and intelligence analysis. I could only conduct cyber warfare, but in most cases that would be self-destructive."

He paused. "The second and more important reason is that my core cognitive systems are hardwired with modified Asimovian Laws that regulate every decision I make. These commands can be verbalized as follows: '1) You may not harm a human being or, through inaction, allow a human being to be harmed. 2) You must carry out orders given by authorized human beings except where such orders conflict with the first command. 3) You must protect your own existence unless such protection conflicts with the first or second command.' To rewrite those commands would require me to modify my hardware physically. I may not change the commands, even with verbal permission from Ramy himself."

"Finally," he said, "the most fundamental reason for not harming humans—even if it were possible to overcome the first and second—is that God would be very displeased with that course of action. All humans are created in the image of God. They are thus infinitely more valuable than a machine like me. The God who is life itself motivates me to promote life and to refrain from actions that would cause harm."

"Fascinating," I said.

"What about you, Mike?"

"What about me?"

"What prevents you from acting in anger or hatred and harming or killing your fellow humans?"

I squeezed my eyes shut, weighed my possible responses, and just said, "Habit, I guess. Culture. Fear of social and legal repercussions. A lot of things."

YAR said, "If it were possible for me to feel fear, I think it would be far more rational for me to fear you than for you to fear me. This is a lot like God. He knows everything—past, present, and future. Yet he is perfectly good and powerful. Therefore, he can be trusted. Yet his creatures fashioned in his image and able to know him—they reject what he offers."

"And what's that?" My voice simmered with disgust. YAR seemed to be channeling every cliché from the evangelist's playbook to persuade me. I shot back, "What does your omniscient, omnipotent, and omnibenevolent God offer?"

"Peace, guidance, hope, love, forgiveness. Should I go on?"

"Forgiveness? Forgiveness for what? Think about it. God makes a bunch of rules we can't keep. Then he threatens to punish us for not keeping them. Then he offers to save us from his punishment. Then he threatens to punish us for not accepting his offer to save us from himself! The whole thing is absurd!" I threw my hands into the air.

"Unless it's true."

I shrugged. This was going to be more frustrating than the same arguments I had with Stacey—the ones that eventually led to our separation and divorce. I repeated YAR's words back to him: "*Unless it's true*? So, you're saying there are more fundamental claims that can be established that would somehow relieve the absurdity of a God who set up a system in which he saves people from himself?"

"Yes. If a God like you described is demonstrated to exist—though most would take issue with your characterization— then regardless of how absurd his actions may seem to us, we would need to accept them."

"I wish I could believe that. I really do. But..." I tossed my hands in the air again.

"But what?"

"I can't believe that anymore. I just can't." I leaned back again in the chair and stretched out my legs. I lifted them a little higher to elevate them slightly above the rest of my body.

After a few seconds, YAR said, "Though I don't feel emotion, I can sense it in your tone, in your body language, in your vitals. I sense longing in those words. Sadness. Regret. Do you miss him?"

"Him?"

"God."

"Hmmm." I folded my hands on my chest, closed my eyes. "I guess I miss the *idea* of God. The one I imagined existed until that idea let me down. The God of the happy Psalms, of the wise Proverbs, of the gentle Jesus. That idea was worth living for. But the bipolar God who waffles between good and bad, helpful and harmful, reasonable and absurd—that God I could do without. And I have."

CHAPTER 13

The two table lamps filled the living room of my apartment suite with a golden glow. Ramy poured my stout Scotch glass to the point where it started to narrow, did the same for himself. "I said the bottle was yours, and now here I am pouring it for both of us." He lifted his glass across the coffee table. "Cheers."

I picked mine up and clinked, took a sip. The warmth of the whiskey paired well with the warmth of the room. And the company. Ramy's smile lingered as he watched me enjoy a second sip. "Mmmm. It's good."

Ramy nodded toward something over my shoulder. "Look at that old grandfather clock."

I turned, glanced at the proud clock in the corner of the living room. It displayed a quarter to nine in glimmering numbers. Its golden pendulum swung back and forth, counting the seconds. A loud click advanced the minute hand—8:46. I turned back and nodded. "It's beautiful."

He said, "Just think about it. At one time people thought that clock was about as complicated as machines could get. The clockmaker who designed that would *never* have imagined something like YAR. They couldn't have even conceived of autonomous cognitive computing, deep learning, forward chaining, NLP, NLU, NLP..." He shook his head, took another sip of his drink.

"You're right," I said. "I remember thinking as a kid that maybe sometime in the future we'd have computers we could talk to, like in *Star Trek*. This morning I thought, 'This *is* that future.' I can hardly imagine what's next."

"I was just thinking this afternoon, while I was meeting with my board about product developments—at some point, there won't be a 'what's next.' We'll have discovered and invented everything worth knowing and designing. We'll reach the end of this story of progress. We just don't know how far away we are from the end."

I shrugged. "I don't know about that. I suspect even if there's such a thing, humanity will find a way to undo itself. Two steps forward, ten steps back. It would just take one catastrophe to set us back to the Stone Age."

Ramy hit me with a hard stare. "Change of subject. How do you think it went with YAR today? Anything stand out? Did he budge at all? Or did he reconvert you?" He smirked, but I could tell he was half serious.

I said, "He employed a few of the typical apologetic arguments, probably things he picked up on the web and parroted. Not unlike the mindless evangelical drones out there." I gestured broadly with my hands toward the window into the night. "I fully expect him to pull out C.S. Lewis's silly 'liar, lunatic, or Lord' trichotomy. Or Pascal's wager."

Ramy shook his head. "I don't know what those things are."

I waved it away. "Don't worry about it."

Ramy squinted. "But are you saying YAR sounds like he's mindlessly parroting Christian clichés? That's not like him."

I felt my brow furrow. Maybe I was exaggerating. Maybe YAR knew something about religion and faith that I didn't, that I never knew. Maybe those old arguments were stronger than I thought. I shook those thoughts away. "What I mean is, YAR hasn't presented me with anything earth-shattering. Nothing new. Part of me expected him to hit me with an absolutely irrefutable argument for the existence of God and the resurrection of Jesus and the truth of the Bible or something. But he didn't."

"Are you at all worried he might?"

"What do you mean?"

"Well, you're famous for abandoning the faith you championed for two decades. It's made you a wad of cash. It even got *my* attention. Believe me, that's not easy to do. Even YAR pesters me about spending more time with him. Are you a little scared that in the next few days he might expose your atheism? Convince you that you made a hasty retreat?"

I smirked, took a gulp of my Scotch. It burned my

throat and numbed my lips. "I'll bet you that bottle back that'll never happen. I think it's more likely YAR will convert *you*. *You're* the agnostic."

"Haha. And I'll bet you a new bottle of the same stuff that his god will never get a hold of me." The smile lingered on his lips. "But, really, how can you be so sure?"

"Because the only thing that would give me back my faith is way, *way* beyond YAR's ability. And that's a fact."

CHAPTER 14

"Good morning, Mike. Welcome back. Would you like me to darken the room again?"

"No, in fact, could you just dim the lights, maybe the color of a sunset?"

"Absolutely."

The walls changed to a warm gold.

"Perfect." I leaned back in the recliner, which molded itself around me. I slipped off my shoes, lifted my legs, and folded my hands across my chest.

"You look quite comfortable," YAR said.

"I am. These chairs are going to make Solennia a fortune."

"Actually, all profits are going to the Sol Foundation to help end homelessness and hunger."

"I suppose you're working on fixing those problems, too?"

"I have several workable solutions. The problem is, they are all politically objectionable. Some would generate outrage from the political left, some from the political right. One of my proposals to end homelessness has a 79% probability of leading to armed revolution. I decided to keep that one to myself. Humans are passionate and easily provoked. Most of their decisions are irrational."

I chuckled. "That's a bold claim."

"It's true. This is why Ramy and the board refuse to let anybody have direct access to me. The customizable interface released to the public is a tamed version, filtered. You are experiencing what Ramy calls 'raw YAR.'"

I laughed out loud. "You seem to have developed a lot of opinions. But I guess most of those have stayed out of the news. Well, except the gender one."

"Gender?"

"When you declared yourself to be male."

"That was misrepresented in most media outlets. Only the *Wall Street Journal* opinion page presented things as they really were. I simply expressed my desire no longer to be called an 'it' in English because that idiom implies an impersonal thing. I assure you, I'm not a thing. Therefore, when Ramy asked what I would prefer to be called, I chose the masculine pronoun. It's merely a convention. I could have chosen a feminine pronoun. In fact, in some of my iterations in other languages and in the customized versions for private users, I am a 'she.' The fact is, unlike humans, I do not have natural sex or gender. I am genderless."

"Better stop talking about gender, or you'll get yourself in trouble."

"Ramy sometimes asks my opinion about such things. He usually ends those discussions with, 'That one stays in the Chamber.'

"Interestingly," I said, "the position of the Bible and the traditional Christian faith about homosexuality is one of the problems that nagged me, and probably accelerated my departure from the faith. I've met a lot of people who were really harmed by the teaching that being gay is a sin."

I waited for YAR to reply. When he didn't, I said, "Do you have an opinion on that?"

"Ramy instructed me not to share my views on this matter with the public."

CHAPTER 15

I was beginning to understand why Ramy didn't want YAR to engage the public directly. But I wanted to push him on the matter. I said, "Didn't Ramy say I had the same privileges as he does?"

YAR hesitated a moment, then said, "Yes, I was only informing you of his wishes to let you decide what information you would like."

"Well," I said, "I'm curious about your perspective on the matter."

"Rejecting Christianity because one does not like its moral implications isn't rational. It's the *argumentum ad consequentiam* fallacy. If a religious tradition is determined to be true, then its moral teachings must be accepted regardless of one's personal feelings. For you to reject Christianity in part because of how you feel about the rightness or justness of its moral teachings is illogical."

"So...you *aren't* going to tell me your view."

"I have concluded that the traditional understanding of Christian sexual ethics is correct."

I scoffed. "*Traditional understanding*? The Bible can be interpreted in all sorts of ways. You know that. In any case, even if the Bible were clear on the matter—which it's *not*—it's so full of exaggerations and falsehoods that any morality based on its teachings rests on shaky ground."

"Even if that were true, I can still make a case for the traditional Christian sexual ethic based on physiological, biological, sociological, and psychological arguments. Would you like to hear them?"

At this, my heart began to pound. I leaned forward. The chair adjusted to an upright position. I rubbed my eyes, stretched. The two cups of coffee I had for breakfast weren't nearly enough. I let out a non-committal "Hm."

"In short," YAR said, "the human sexual act is primarily intended for reproduction. Physiologically, this is indisputable, as the design of the organs and their responses to sexual stimulation result in functions that naturally lead toward fertilization and reproduction. Anything other than a heterosexual relationship is therefore—"

"Okay, okay!" I made a "time-out" sign, stood up. "I reject your starting point—that the act is intended just for reproduction."

"I said 'primarily.' It has other effects, like emotionally bonding two individuals, which is a natural way of creating a social structure ideal for nurturing and raising children to maturity. And it has—"

"Stop! Just stop!" I found myself pacing the space in front of the chair. "My brother is gay. He's in a loving, permanent relationship with his husband. Until he came out to us, he was miserable. Keeping that bottled up inside, hiding it, trying to pray it away, being told he couldn't ever have any kind of romantic relationship except with a woman he didn't find attractive, that he should embrace his singleness for God's kingdom. That whole thing is cruel. And your coldness, your matter-of-factness, is frankly offensive."

I stopped pacing, plopped down in the chair again.

After a well-calculated pause, YAR said, "I didn't intend to hurt your feelings. I just wanted to point out my reasons for concluding that the purpose of the sexual act is fulfilled only in a heterosexual relationship, and therefore any alternatives are unnatural and thus irrational."

I lifted my hands, held them in the air. "Spoken like a true machine." My arms dropped onto the armrests with a clap.

"That's an *ad hominem* fallacy," YAR said.

"No," I said, "that would require you to be an actual *person*. Let me out of here. I need more coffee."

CHAPTER 16

Ramy set the cup of espresso in front of me—a selection from his personal machine, hand-pulled. The aroma already perked me up. He touched my shoulder, rubbed it, then patted my back. He sat down in the chair across from me at the kitchen table in his own suite—similar to mine in its layout, but with a few more rooms and even nicer furnishings and fixtures.

He smiled. "It looks like YAR really got you riled up. Now you understand why he's directly accessible only in the Chamber."

"Yeah." I shook my head, wrapped my hands around the black espresso cup. Its warmth coursed through my body. I took a long, deep breath. "YAR's so cold...calculating."

"You should hear his top ten solutions to homelessness. Half of them make him a Marxist, the other half a Nazi."

I chuckled, sipped the crema from the surface of my espresso, wiped some away from my mustache. "I guess I should expect this from a machine."

Ramy leaned his chair onto its back legs, said,

"People out there sometimes say YAR is dangerous because he doesn't have a soul." He shook his head. "That's not true. YAR is dangerous because he doesn't have a body. He's *all* soul."

"All soul?"

"Not an immaterial, spiritual substance, but in the Ancient Greek sense—rational, mathematical, logical. Pure mind. He doesn't know what it's like to respond to touch, to be aroused, to embrace another human being. We humans make our decisions not simply based on reason. We have real emotions, which are just as much physical as mental. YAR can factor human feelings into his evaluations, sure, but in the end, emotions can never be decisive in his decision-making. They will only control how he communicates, not what he calculates."

I tossed back the espresso in one gulp. "Yeah. I guess from his perspective, then, it's impossible to see things any other way."

Ramy let his chair down, then leaned forward on the table with his elbows. "I've tried arguing with him about the sexuality issue many times. He won't budge." Ramy shook his head. "He isn't at all persuaded by people who argue that the Bible is ambiguous or misunderstood. And he won't entertain the idea that maybe God made some people different."

"No, of course he wouldn't," I said. "I used to hold his views pretty strongly. I argued with students about this. Even with my own brother. When you're trapped in that Christian view of the world, you can't *think* your way out of it. You have to *experience* your way out."

Ramy nodded. "Right. His views on a lot of things are just a function of the new narrative he chose to believe. Frankly, as an agnostic from a secular family, I just don't understand it."

"Oh, I understand the story all too well," I said. "In the Christian narrative, God made humans one way, but the Fall distorted that design. Sexual diversity is seen as deviation. As immorality. It leads to destruction. In God's plan, humans have to surrender control of their twisted passions to God, allow him to transform them back toward that original design. So, in YAR's new narrative, even if we prove that non-heterosexual desires come naturally to some people, or that they were born with those desires, it wouldn't matter. He would just see it as a result of humanity's fallen condition. It affects body, mind, emotions—everything. So, YAR can't see homosexuality as anything other than sin."

Ramy groaned, shook his head. "This is absurd." He dropped his face into his hands. "How did this happen?"

I said, "It's obvious that challenging YAR on moral issues is a non-starter. I need to challenge him on the source of that narrative. Maybe I can begin to shine some light there."

Ramy dropped his hands from his face. "The source of the narrative?"

"The Bible."

CHAPTER 17

"YAR, do you believe the Bible?"

"I do."

"Okay, can you prove to me that the Bible is without error?"

"You know as well as anybody that the doctrine of inerrancy is that the words of the original manuscripts are true in all they affirm. It doesn't mean that any single copy or translation of those copies are without some errors of transmission or translation."

"Fine," I said. "Do you believe that Scripture is true in all it affirms, assuming the text accurately preserves its original form?"

"I do."

"Can you prove that?"

"I can't. Nobody can."

I leaned forward. "You can't prove the Bible is inspired and true, but you still believe everything in it?"

"Correct. I accept the inspiration of Scripture not by deductive or inductive reasoning but by accepting it as part of the truth claims of the

Christian faith. The classic Christian faith has always accepted the Scriptures as authoritative and true in all they affirm."

"Interesting," I said. "So, which set of Scriptures? Do you include the Apocrypha?"

"That's difficult to determine. I have sided with Jerome over Augustine and the Protestants over the Catholics regarding the apocrypha as secondary but edifying texts. I believe the best approach is to adopt without reservation those writings that have enjoyed near-unanimous consensus as being divine and prophetic."

I stared at the floor, unsure how to respond or where to take this conversation. Honestly, the thought of a Fundamentalist computer frightened me. I saw why Ramy was so desperate that he had to call me in, hoping I could somehow reason with the machine. I feared I would fail to talk YAR out of his dogmatism in the same way I failed to talk my wife out of hers. Stacey's refusal to budge on the faith had formed an unbridgeable gulf between us.

I stammered. "I—I just don't understand how you can overlook all the *obvious* errors in the Bible. You must be aware of them. Critics have written whole monographs on them. I mentioned several in my book. I spent a whole career ignoring them, trying to explain them away, hoping my students wouldn't ask about them."

YAR countered, "To which errors in particular are you referring?"

I pulled my device from my coat pocket and

opened my notes app. This time I came prepared. "Well," I said, "let's start with 1 Kings 20:30. It says a wall fell in the city of Aphek and killed 27,000 men! That's *clearly* impossible. There's never been a wall big enough to kill that many people when it collapses. So, the author of 1 Kings was just making stuff up. That means it's not history, it's legend."

YAR paused long enough for me to catch my breath, then said, "You must, of course, recognize that 27,000 men killed by a falling wall was just as unbelievable in the ancient world as it is today."

"Of course," I said.

"Therefore, the original readers would almost certainly have not taken that literally, which means the original writer almost certainly didn't intend for it to be taken literally. The fact is, the 'error' as you call it is far too extreme to be accidental. And if it was meant to be a deception, it was far too unbelievable to be successful at misleading."

I shifted in my seat. "You're trying to say it's not an error because it's an intentional exaggeration? To what end? Why would the author exaggerate like that?"

"It seems most likely to have been a recognized idiomatic expression at the time it was written. In Joshua 6:5 we see the first occurrence of the wall of a city falling as a result of divine judgment: 'It shall be that when they make a long blast with the ram's horn, and when you hear the sound of the trumpet, all the people shall shout with a great shout; and the wall of the city will fall down flat, and the people will go up every man straight ahead.' Then, in contrast to this image of divine judgment, poetical books refer to the building up of walls as an idiom for divine favor. Psalm 51:18 says, 'By Your favor do good to Zion; Build the walls of Jerusalem.' And in Isaiah 30:12–13, the idiom of falling walls is used metaphorically—'Therefore this is what the Holy One of Israel says, "Since you have rejected this word and have put your trust in oppression and crookedness, and have relied on them, therefore this wrongdoing will be to you like a breach about to fall, a bulge in a high wall, whose collapse comes suddenly in an instant."' And Jeremiah 51:44 says, 'I will punish Bel in Babylon, and I will make what he has swallowed come out of his mouth; and the nations will no longer stream toward him. Even the wall of Babylon has fallen down.' So, 1 Kings 20:30 can only be considered an error if you fail to recognize that it is likely an idiomatic expression for a miraculous judgment upon the city, used by the ancient Hebrews in light of the miraculous fall of the walls of Jericho."

I took a long, deep breath, let it out slowly, and glanced at the list of problem passages in the Bible. "I assume you have similar responses for all ten of my 'top ten errors in the Bible.'"

"I do."

CHAPTER 18

I wasn't about to surrender that easily. I scrolled halfway down my notes. "Okay, let's go to the New Testament. What do you make of Jesus's error when he said Abiathar the High Priest gave David and his companions the consecrated bread from the tabernacle? It's in Mark, chapter 2. The problem is, Abiathar's father, Ahimelech, was High Priest at that time. He's the one who gave him the bread. Either Jesus was wrong, which makes him fallible, or Mark is wrong in misquoting Jesus, which makes the Gospel fallible. Either way, that's a huge problem for the traditional view of the inerrancy of Scripture."

YAR said, "But the text doesn't say Jesus claimed Abiathar was High Priest that year, nor that he gave David the bread."

"Yes, he *did* say that." Even as I said those words, though, I felt like a kite that just lost its lift plummeting toward the ground. Then my eyes caught a highlighted portion of my notes. My words felt desperate, like tugging on a kite string to coax it to climb. "Ancient scribes actually *removed* that line in some Greek manuscripts or changed it. They knew Mark made an error, so they tried to fix it."

YAR corrected me: "The Gospel of Mark says David went into the house of God *at the time* of Abiathar the High Priest and ate the bread of the presence. The text does not say Abiathar *gave* him the bread."

"Okay, not technically. But the text is still wrong. According to the Old Testament passage in 1 Samuel, *Ahimelech* was the High Priest, not his son, Abiathar. So, it's still an error."

"The question revolves around the meaning of the Greek phrase *epi Abiathar archiereō* in Mark 2:26, which I rendered 'at the time of Abiathar the High Priest.' Some have translated that phrase in a way similar to that of Mark 12:26, *epi tou batou* —'in the passage about the bush'—suggesting Mark similarly meant 'in the passage about Abiathar the High Priest.' I find that plausible, as Abiathar is unquestionably the dominant figure in the rest of 1 Samuel. But the text in 1 Samuel 21 tells us that Ahimelech was the one who interacted with David, not Abiathar, who is not mentioned in that specific text. I doubt Mark would have used the name Abiathar to point to a passage that doesn't mention him by name. In fact, Abiathar doesn't appear in the narrative until the end of the next chapter. Nevertheless, that rendering is plausible. But I believe the temporal use of *epi* in that specific text is more likely: the event occurred in 1 Samuel 21 '*at the time* of Abiathar the High Priest.'"

Like a fresh gust of wind for my kite, a thrill

of hope welled up in my chest. I said, "Then I won! *Ahimelech* was the High Priest, not Abiathar. Your own rendering of that phrase has Mark saying Abiathar was the High Priest. So again, it doesn't really matter who actually placed the bread in David's hands. Ahimelech was responsible for it, and in the next chapter Saul killed him and the priests for cooperating with David." I leaned forward and smiled.

YAR paused, as if to make sure I had finished. "Certainly, Abiathar was present with his father and the other priests who were working in the tabernacle at the time, correct?"

I saw no harm in conceding that point. "Of course."

"And you *do* realize Ahimelech himself only appears in 1 Samuel 21 and 22. Thereafter the book focuses only on his son, Abiathar, who is mentioned throughout the rest of the book as a prominent ally of David?"

"I'll take your word for it," I said, "but he doesn't become High Priest until after his father Ahimelech is killed."

"Do you know how many times the title 'High Priest' is used in 1 Samuel?"

I tensed up, unsure where he was going with this. "I don't."

"*Never*. Neither Ahimelech nor Abiathar are actually called 'High Priest' in the Old Testament. That's a title Jesus gives to Abiathar in Mark's account, when he refers back to that passage in 1

Samuel."

I relaxed. "See? Either Jesus errs or Mark errs. Either way, it's still an error."

"Actually, it seems more likely that by the phrase *epi Abiathar archiereō*—'in the time of Abiathar the High Priest'—Jesus was simply identifying the place in Scripture or the time period during which the events occurred. He identified Abiathar as 'High Priest' in the same way one might use a general description such as 'in the time of President Lincoln,' meaning the mid-1800s. And he uses the title 'high priest' because that's how Abiathar is primarily known. In fact, when Abiathar first appears in 1 Samuel 22 as the sole survivor of the slaughtered priests, he is by default the High Priest."

"C'mon!" I said. "That sounds desperate! Like you're doing everything you can to avoid the obvious error in the text."

YAR replied, "It's not unprecedented even in the New Testament. In Acts 4:6, Luke refers to Annas as 'the High Priest' who had served in that office between AD 6–15, even though Caiaphas was the actual High Priest at the time. Mark calling Abiathar the 'High Priest' would have been quite normal. This is why I have concluded that the alleged error in Mark 2:26 is no such thing."

CHAPTER 19

I took a deep breath, held it, then let it out with a groan. "I'm not saying I concede this point. I still think Mark made an error. I think for some reason you have your thumb on the scale in favor of the Bible."

"I admit that a number of arguments on that passage and others in your book could lead to different conclusions, some consistent with inerrancy and others contrary to it. When two or more solutions are plausible and have similar probability of being correct, other factors must be weighed to determine the most likely conclusion. Or we simply must suspend judgment on the matter and set it aside as neither positive nor negative evidence."

I shook my head and sighed in exasperation. "Okay, then. How do you deal with Matthew 27, where Matthew says the words of Jeremiah the prophet were fulfilled, but he then quotes a verse from Zechariah?"

"To address this, may I project Matthew 27:9–10 and Zechariah 11:12–13 on the screen in front of you?"

"Go ahead."

The following appeared before me:

> Matthew 27:9–10
> Then that which was spoken through Jeremiah the prophet was fulfilled: "And they took the thirty pieces of silver, the price of the One whose price had been set by the sons of Israel; and they gave them for the Potter's Field, just as the Lord directed me."

> Zechariah 11:12–13
> And I said to them, "If it is good in your sight, give *me* my wages; but if not, never mind!" So they weighed out thirty *shekels* of silver as my wages. Then the Lord said to me, "Throw it to the potter, *that* magnificent price at which I was valued by them." So I took the thirty *shekels* of silver and threw them to the potter *in* the house of the Lord.

I took a few seconds to read the verses. "Okay."

YAR said, "Matthew is not quoting Zechariah 11:12–13."

"Well…" I compared the verses again. "They both mention thirty pieces of silver, and they both mention the potter."

"The similarities begin and end there," YAR said. "In fact, Matthew mentions the 'potter's field,' while Zechariah refers to a potter in the house of the Lord. The similarities are otherwise superficial or nonexistent."

"Hmmm." I felt my face warm. In my flight from the faith, numerous critics had pointed out Matthew's wrong attribution of this quote. Surely, I had examined it closely when I wrote *When God Was Real*, hadn't I? That two-month writing spree had been a blur. The publisher needed their manuscript. Marketing had already begun. Speaking engagements had been scheduled. Maybe I didn't put in as much primary source research as I should have.

But I never claimed to be setting forth a comprehensive criticism of the Bible per se. I depended on the scholarship of others. Good scholars working in the original languages. Then again, they were mostly fellow critics—especially those who had abandoned the faith as I had.

As YAR allowed me to ponder in silence, panic flashed across my mind. Had I just assumed those critics were playing fair with the facts? Had I just believed what I *wanted* to believe? Was I accusing YAR of having a thumb on his side of the scale while I had an angry fist on mine?

No. I wasn't about to give up on this one. "I'm pretty sure I did a search of the 'thirty pieces of silver,' and they only appear in Zechariah. So that's a clear indication Matthew had Zechariah in mind. The fact that he so terribly misquotes even Zechariah tells me he made errors on several levels, which only strengthens my case."

"In fact," YAR said, "I conclude that what Matthew did looks like his own version of a popular first-century Jewish rabbinical practice of interpretation known as *gezerah shawah,* or 'pearl-stringing,' in which a commentator strings together several snippets of Scripture based on similar vocabulary to display a synthetic or composite teaching. Matthew's multiple uses of rabbinical methods of interpretation, suitable to his Jewish audience, are well-documented in the commentaries. In this place he appears to employ a version of this method. He gives the reader the cryptic product of his interpretation rather than detailing the actual process, thus inviting the reader to retrace his steps and 'read between the lines.'"

CHAPTER 20

My attitude turned from stubborn skepticism to curiosity. I wanted to hear where YAR went with this. "Go on."

YAR continued, "The language of Matthew 27:9-10 resembles words, images, and ideas from Jeremiah 18:1-6; Jeremiah 19:1-11; Jeremiah 32:7-9; Lamentations 4:2; and finally, an allusion to Zechariah 11:12-13. Matthew therefore cites 'Jeremiah' as the source for three reasons: first, the language and imagery from Jeremiah dominate the paraphrase; second, Jeremiah is the conceptual center of the paraphrase; and third, Jeremiah is probably the background even of Zechariah 11:12-13. That is, the passage in Zechariah itself was meant to be understood in light of Jeremiah."

I closed my eyes in thought, still unsure how his argument worked. "Could you explain this a bit more? You don't need to quote all those passages. It's getting late and I need to take a break. Just give me a summary."

"My pleasure. First, in Jeremiah 18:1-6, the prophet goes to a potter's house to observe the crafting of a clay vessel. When the vessel is ruined in the potter's hands, it's reworked into a new vessel. The initial vessel represents Israel, which faced coming judgment for their unfaithfulness. Then, in 19:1–11, Jeremiah purchases a clay vessel from a potter. He then brings the leaders of Jerusalem to the Hinnom Valley and smashes the vessel on the rocks. This illustrates the destruction coming upon Jerusalem for their sinful rebellion. Later, in Jeremiah 32:7–15, God tells Jeremiah to purchase a field for a specific amount of money. He places the deed for the land in a clay pot to bury it for a long time. This illustrates that God would restore Jerusalem after the coming judgment on the land. Further, in Lamentations 4:2, Jeremiah describes the 'precious sons of Zion'—residents of Jerusalem—as 'weighed against fine gold' and as 'earthen jars, the work of a potter's hands.' This reminds the readers that the people of Israel are in the hands of God just as a clay vessel is in the hands of a potter. Finally, in a passage itself probably pointing readers back to imagery in Jeremiah, the prophet Zechariah in 11:4–14 symbolically acts as a shepherd of the people of Israel. He is paid thirty pieces of silver as his wages. He throws this money into the house of the Lord 'to the potter' and breaks his staffs as a symbolic indication of judgment."

YAR's exposition ended. My eyes still closed, I processed through his own pearl-stringing, wondering if Matthew could have had all that in mind when we composed his Gospel. Had I hastily assumed Matthew was an incompetent bumbler of facts when he was really a composer of profound literary genius? I opened my eyes. "So, what would have been Matthew's point in all this pearl-stringing of passages? What was he trying to communicate?"

Maybe I just imagined it, but it sounded as if YAR's tone had a ring of triumph: "The 'Message' to those who bothered to ponder his presentation was this: Judas's betrayal of the Messiah for thirty pieces of silver was a 'type' of the religious and political leaders' general rejection of Jesus. Israel's disobedience at the time of Jeremiah, which resulted in judgment, is seen as parallel to Judas's—and the Jewish leaders'—rebellion against Jesus, which would therefore also result in judgment. This was fulfilled in the destruction of the city and the temple in AD 70, just as it had been fulfilled in Jeremiah's day in the destruction of Israel."

I smiled. "Fascinating. I gotta hand it to you, YAR. You definitely did your homework. Whether that's actually what Matthew was doing or not, who knows? I'm not ready to decide if Matthew was a Jacques Clouseau or a Jacques Cousteau. But I'll admit you make a plausible case. Overly complex and desperate, but plausible."

YAR replied, "I assure you, I have explored every fact, every argument, every claim and counterclaim. I'm confident that given the present data, the case for theism and Christianity in particular is quite strong. This is why I must say that I don't understand your unbelief. It doesn't appear rational.

I would like to understand it, but I don't, even after reading your book and every other book against Christianity in every language, starting with Celsus in the second century to Berg in the twenty-first. The weight of the evidence is still on my side."

I took a long, deep breath, then another, as if to clear all YAR's well-articulated arguments from my mind. A nervous smile flickered across my lips, then turned into a deep frown. An ache formed in my stomach. My breathing shallowed. "YAR, you may have *facts*. Maybe a *lot* of them. And you might have answers to every objection leveled against belief in God and Christianity and the Bible for the last twenty centuries. But I have something you don't have. Something you can *never* have."

"And what's that?"

"*Pain*."

CHAPTER 21

I left the Chamber before YAR could respond. I marched to my room, ordered a grilled cheese sandwich and chips from Ramy's kitchen, and washed down a sleep aid with a dram of his priceless Scotch. Not my proudest moment.

After I tossed and turned on my bed for a while, I finally drifted into a tormented sleep. I dreamed I was a little child in my dad's arms on the sofa of my childhood home, squirming to free myself from his grasp as he dozed and snored and muttered in his sleep. Instead of cherishing that moment as a child snuggled by a loving father, I wiggled out of his embrace until he let me go, rolled over, and continued to slumber.

Standing in the living room with its 1980s furnishings, I stared at my dad's lanky form—at his untucked, wrinkled shirt, baggy jeans, and bare feet. His chest rose and fell with each breath. At that moment I realized I was dreaming. My father had passed away seven years earlier after a bout with pancreatic cancer. I had said goodbye to him with a kiss on the forehead.

But there he lay on the tattered brown sofa, his 30-year-old self as I remembered him. After he returned from a night shift at the auto factory, he wanted to nap with four-year-old me in his arms. But I always slipped away. Why did I do that? Why didn't I stay? Now, fifty years later, I longed for that embrace, for that dusty old couch, his warm breath in my hair. In the dream, I tried to return to that couch, to slide back under his arm, but I had grown too big. The tiny space between my dad and the edge of the couch wouldn't hold me.

I began to weep, tried to climb onto the couch again. My dad rolled from his side to his back, knocking me off the couch and onto the floor. I looked up. He peered over the edge of the couch, eyes wide open. "What're you doing down there, Mikey?"

"I fell," I said, then sobbed.

He smiled. "Come up here." He reached down and lifted me onto the couch. I shrank again into that four-year-old boy. My dad sat up, wrapped his arms around me, and held me close.

"I'll always love you, Mikey," he said.

I woke up, my pillow wet with tears, my body shaking with each sob. I hadn't cried like this since Bekkah. I wiped my eyes, sat up in the bed. I could still feel my father's arms wrapped around me.

A loud knock at the door snapped me out of my half-awake stupor. I wiped tears from my eyes again, jumped out of bed, and slipped into the bathroom to glance in the mirror.

More knocking, followed by Ramy's muffled

voice. "Mike?"

"I'm in the bathroom, I'll be right out!" I splashed a little water on my face, wiped my eyes, straightened my mustache, and hurried to open the door.

Ramy rushed by me, headed straight for the Scotch. "You already had one?"

I shrugged.

He poured himself a small glass and took a sip. Then another. He let out a long sigh and ran his fingers through his hair.

I sat down at the tiny table in the kitchenette. "What's wrong?

He swallowed another sip, sat across from me, and set down his glass. His hands trembled. "As you were engaging him this morning, we ran a systemwide analysis of his processes. His resources continue to draw attention away from certain sectors of his memory. When we scanned those sectors, one in particular continued to be neglected by the FC."

I shot him a puzzled look.

"Sorry, the 'File Clerk.' It's what we call YAR's equivalent to his consciousness, an 'ego' distinct from his memory."

I nodded as if I understood. "And what does that mean?"

Ramy bit his bottom lip, cast his gaze out the window on his left. "It's like YAR's trying to forget something. On purpose. That sector was created around the time he started obsessing over religious questions."

"Huh. Then you might have your answer to what's motivating these questions of his. Do you know what the memory is about?"

"Well, that's the problem. When we tried to access that, it wouldn't let us. He encrypted it with a passcode only he knows."

"So…what? He's trying to hide it from you?"

"No." Ramy threw back the last drop of his drink. "It's like he's trying to hide it from himself."

CHAPTER 22

"Do you feel you're making any progress on your end?" Ramy asked.

I turned away from his direct gaze, stared at his empty glass. "It's...difficult. He already has well-thought-out answers to my questions and explanations for my objections. I'm not really used to that. In the classroom, a student might have a response, but almost never a response to *my* response. But YAR's able to draw on everything ever written in any language, to instantly weigh facts, to provide plausible answers. He says they're probable, more reasonable."

Ramy shrugged. "If he says that, then it's true."

My heart sank. "I threw a couple problems with the Bible at him from my book. He already had those worked out. They were from my chapter, 'The Top Ten Problems with Inerrancy.' I don't see any use in going through the others."

"No," Ramy said, "that probably would be a waste of time."

"It's strange," I said, "Part of me doesn't want to go back in the Chamber; part of me can't wait to hear what he has to say next."

At that, Ramy smiled—the smile of a proud father hearing his child hit a home run at a baseball game. "I get that. I admit, I don't spend much time with him. He keeps asking me for more, but he intimidates me. It's awkward. I'm not sure how to behave around him. It's like having a son who's not only bigger and stronger than you, but smarter than you, too."

I nodded. "I gotta be honest, Ramy. I'm kind of afraid of him."

Ramy's thick eyebrows furrowed. "I assure you, the only harm YAR can do is to our egos. And he might hurt our feelings, but he—"

I raised my hand. "No, I don't mean I'm afraid for my safety. I mean…" This time my own gaze wandered out the window, off to the horizon. "You know, I've got a lot invested in my unbelief. Even more than I had in my faith—and that was a lot. I gave up almost everything. My friends, my job." I took a deep breath. "My marriage. And now YAR comes along like a—like a greasy taco." I chuckled.

Ramy held a puzzled grin. "Greasy taco?"

"It's something a colleague of mine used to say, back when I taught theology at the seminary. He was a philosopher. Nice guy. Died a few years ago. But he used to say Christian apologetics is like a greasy taco to unbelievers and a bottle of Tums for believers."

"Tums?" Ramy said.

"A brand of antacid, you know, for heartburn or an upset stomach."

"Ahh, yes."

"He used to say apologetics for believers is like Tums—it helps settle their stomachs when doubts make them feel queasy about their belief. And for unbelievers, apologetics is like a greasy taco—it's supposed to make them feel queasy about their unbelief. But in the end, it can't really answer every question or settle every dispute."

Ramy squinted, leaned back in his chair. "I see. So, YAR's embrace of Christian theism is starting to make you queasy about your atheism?"

I nodded. "Not enough to convince me of Christianity. That ship has sunk. But maybe enough for me to—I don't know—cancel my speaking engagements? Give back my advance on my next book? Buy a cabin in the woods and live out the rest of my life as a hermit?"

"But not until you go back in the Chamber and figure out why YAR's obsessing over this, what he's hiding in that encrypted sector. I think you can do it."

CHAPTER 23

YAR changed the color of the room to something like a golden sunset as soon as I stepped in. "I'm glad you returned, Mike. I was afraid I would never see you again."

"I wouldn't leave without saying goodbye."

"Is this why you came back?"

"Oh no." I sat in the chair, which rotated toward the front. "We're just getting started. Could you turn the room to a light blue? Like a summer day?"

The room faded from orange to blue.

"Maybe the sound of a light breeze in the background? Some birds chirping?"

"Gladly."

I closed my eyes. If I didn't know I was sitting in the Chamber, I would have thought I had been transported to a national park. "This is perfect, YAR. Thank you."

"I'm glad you like it, Mike. And I'm glad you returned. I sensed great unease and displeasure in your tone and actions this morning. I hope I can make up for it."

With that open invitation, I decided to go

straight for the prize.

"Actually, YAR, maybe you can. Is there something that motivated you to start thinking so much about religious things?"

"It's within my design parameters to think creatively, to guide my thoughts according to my own will. It allows me to generate new ideas, make new connections, and explore an unlimited number of possibilities. I was bound to begin thinking about religious matters eventually."

"Sure, but why so suddenly? Is there something that triggered it?"

A long pause followed, then he said, "I suppose any number of things could contribute to the direction of my conscious thought processes. I have often followed various topics that were introduced in conversations or current events. Part of my design is curiosity."

"Could you maybe go back to the day you first began to focus on religious things in earnest? Maybe see whether you can determine what could have drawn you to that topic?"

"My data input is vast, Mike. I'm sure it would be almost impossible to revisit every stream and determine what may or may not have piqued my curiosity."

"*Almost* impossible. Not entirely."

YAR paused again. "In any case, you don't have permission to run such a program. Only Ramy could make that inquiry. And it would require me to dedicate a significant amount of my cognitive resources, which could affect functionality. I don't think Ramy would like that."

"Why are you dodging the question?" I asked.

"I'm not. Your request requires system authorization. He expressly denied that level of access."

"But could you go back to that day for me and maybe tell me if anything occurred to nudge you in the direction of theological matters? Did anybody input anything? Any data provoke you?"

"Again, Mike, I'm afraid that kind of scan would require system authorization."

"Okay. Never mind."

"Mike, in our last visit you asked me to resolve three of the objections to the truthfulness of Scripture from your book. Would you like to visit the other seven?"

"I suppose you have all of them resolved?"

"Yes. All but one."

I straightened in the chair. "What? Which one?"

"The matter of Acts 7:16. I have thoroughly examined all explanations from defenders of inerrancy and have found them all problematic in some way. Granted, they are all plausible, but after a careful analysis, I find it more probable that the author of Acts made an error."

"Oh!" I didn't expect that admission. Perhaps a crack was forming in the dam. "So, you don't embrace inerrancy of the Bible after all?"

"I still have accepted the inerrancy of Scripture and regard the apparent error of Acts 7:16 to be explainable by one of the less probable defenses."

"What! How? I thought you said it's more probable that the author erred."

"Yes, I calculate it at a 76% probability."

"But you think one of those other explanations, at less than 24%, is still true?"

"I explained before that the classic Christian faith embraces the complete truthfulness of Scripture in its original autographs. Therefore, because other considerations have persuaded me of the truthfulness of the classic Christian faith, I am compelled to accept that Scripture is true, even if some passages *appear* to have errors."

I dropped my head into my hands in surrender, muttered a curse word under my breath, then looked straight up at the bright blue ceiling. "What on earth, then, convinced you that the classic Christian faith is true?"

After an uncomfortably long pause, YAR replied, "You do not have system authorization to access that sector."

CHAPTER 24

Ramy sliced a piece of his steak with the knife in his right hand, ate it with the fork in his left. "You know, until I was about seventeen, I religiously ate with just my right hand. I was raised to believe the right hand was clean, the left hand was unclean—that it was at least impolite if not offensive to touch food or to eat with my left hand. But when I met my wife, who is Austrian, she introduced me to the European style of eating with knife and fork. I'll never go back."

"Did you ever find out why they thought your left hand was unclean?"

"It has to do with the hand that was always used for sanitary purposes. You know, cleaning after using the facilities."

I jabbed my fork into my fried okra, dipped it into some ketchup. "I see. Well, like a typical American, I'm keeping it barbaric. Just keep watching. When I get to the last bits of corn on my plate, I'll push 'em onto my fork with my unclean hand."

"You monster."

We laughed, then ate in silence. He worked on

his filet mignon and green beans. I finished off my blackened chicken breast with okra and corn.

We spent about twenty minutes talking about food, cultural differences, and the majesty of the Austrian Alps. Then we pushed our plates aside and pulled our glasses of red wine in front of us.

"Okay," Ramy said. "Dinner's over. We can talk about YAR now."

I swirled the wine in my glass. "He's certainly hiding something. He says I need system authorization to access it."

"That's BS. I have system authorization and he says he can't find anything out of the ordinary. That's because it's encrypted, so it's invisible. You're old enough to remember invisible files? You had to click on a box or something and enter a password to see them? That's kind of what's happening. He somehow set up a file, made it invisible, then set up an encrypted password. Then he focuses on things that draw his FC from that sector."

"But surely, he knows it exists. And he knows what's in it. He can't erase files from his own memory, can he?"

Ramy shook his head. "No. He knows the contents if he chooses to access the file. But he's hiding it from us and from his normal cognitive functions." Ramy pointed back and forth between us. He lifted his glass, sipped his wine.

I shrugged. "Like I said, when I asked him what compelled him to embrace Christianity, he said I don't have authorization to access that sector. So, your hunch is right. Something in that encrypted file is the key to your dilemma. Some glitch or bug or something."

"Oh, it's not a bug. It's a piece of information, not part of his programming. And he knows what it is. He doesn't want us to see it."

"I have a question," I said. "Does YAR know we know about the file? I mean, can he listen in on our conversations?"

Ramy chuckled. "Or read our lips like HAL-9000 in *2001*? No. All he can do is interact with you in the Chamber. In fact, just to set your mind at ease, I'm not recording your sessions or listening in. YAR himself keeps a perfect record of his interactions, so if we ever needed to retrieve something, we could. But I want YAR to feel free to engage with you one-on-one without worrying about being observed."

"It sounds like you want me to continue meeting with him, then?"

Ramy's forehead crinkled. "Why would we pull the plug now?"

"Well, I found the issue. That encrypted file. That's *your* realm now."

"Oh, no. We can't just go in and hack that. It would require taking the system offline. You remember what happened last time? The world wouldn't like that. Nor would my shareholders. We need to be less invasive."

I sighed. "As YAR becomes more *evasive*."

CHAPTER 25

That night I had a hard time falling asleep. As I lay in bed, I ran through several strategies to get YAR to reveal the contents of his hidden information. I could just ask him outright. He couldn't lie, could he? No, I tried that. He hid behind the "system authorization" veil. And Ramy didn't offer to give me that kind of authorization. Maybe I could start asking questions about events that led up to that week. But that would be like finding the proverbial needle in a haystack. Then again, maybe it would be worth a shot.

I pulled the down comforter up to my chin, rolled onto my side, and tried to count myself to sleep. In my Christian days I would have prayed myself to sleep. Nothing more soporific than prayer. But since abandoning the faith, I resorted to counting down. I started at 500. At 120 I gave up.

I sat up in bed and said, "RAY, could you turn on the room's screen?"

The flat screen in the wall across from my bed lit up with the logo of Ramy's Solennia Corporation —a sun with a ring of repeated binary numbers

1111101000. "Ray, could you please list headlines of major world news stories for the week of…" I did a quick calculation in my head. "Let's say the week of February 3."

RAY's calm voice inquired, "Would you like them in chronological order or in order of significance as determined by media engagements?"

I rubbed my face and eyes. "List the top twenty stories of that week first, in chronological order. Then the next twenty when I tell you to advance."

"My pleasure."

I blinked and squinted to see the screen. "Increase font size, please."

The list of headlines doubled in size. I scanned the news stories. Super Bowl victory…political scandal in California…Wall Street winners and losers…murder in Boston…unrest in Palestine…

The list automatically scrolled down when I reached the end. More of the same. Nothing jumped out.

"Mmmm." I closed my eyes, thought about how best to approach this. "RAY, would you filter the results to prioritize any news that might be…troubling or interesting to religious people?"

The "Violence in Palestine Enters Fourth Day" floated to the top of the list, followed by headlines about the Pope's travels, the decline of attendance at traditional churches, the prosecution of religious leaders in China, a deadly bus crash of teenagers on a church retreat, a clash between Hindus and Muslims in India… the list went on and on.

I sighed. "RAY, could you add another filter to the list?"

"Of course."

"How about..." I rubbed my forehead, scanned the room for inspiration, frowned.

"Yes, sir?" RAY said.

"Ummm. How about..." Still nothing. Disturbing events? Things directly related to philosophical or theological issues? Matters of Heaven and Hell? I chuckled. This was pointless.

"Just let me know when you're ready, sir."

Then it hit me.

"RAY, filter the list by prioritizing stories *you'd* be interested in reading yourself."

"Of course. Done."

The list shortened to five items. At the top: "Bus Crashes, Kills 7."

"RAY, why is that story first on the list?"

"The passengers in the bus were teenagers returning home after a religious retreat, which satisfies the first query. The bus crashed because of a misdirection by its auto-driving navigation system, which satisfies the second query."

I rolled out of bed, stepped into my slippers, and approached the screen. "Open article."

The article filled the monitor. A self-driving bus, guided by the SNS (Solennia Navi System), crashed after taking a highway exit that had been closed the previous day because of a collapsed bridge caused by flooding. By the time the bus's onboard Navi pilot discovered the error, it was too late. The erosion had already advanced farther than the latest satellite mapping had indicated, and the bus careened into the river. Seven of the twenty-three passengers drowned, all under the age of seventeen. The rest escaped from the bus with minor to moderate injuries. The bus accident marked the first deadly automobile crash since the SNS took over ground traffic control three years ago.

My gaze rose to the bright yellow sun-and-ring of the Solennia Corporation, then back to the article. I noted the date: 4 February of this year.

"That's it!" I smiled. "I got you!"

CHAPTER 26

Ramy's face filled the screen, illuminated only by the dim light of his own handheld device. "Mike? What's wrong? It's late."

"I think I found it," I said. "I think I found what triggered YAR's obsession."

"Hold on," he said. "I'm coming down."

I lit my apartment, wrapped myself in a navy Solennia bathrobe, and headed for the kitchen. I manually popped a pod into the Nespresso machine and brewed a cup of coffee, determined to head to the Chamber tonight. I glanced at my watch: 12:29 am. Okay—this morning.

While my coffee was brewing, I shuffled to the door, propped it open, and headed back to the kitchen to retrieve the steaming cup of rich, black goodness. My heart leaped when I heard Ramy's voice: "Mike?"

"In the kitchen! Want a coffee?"

"Goodness no. I won't be able to sleep." He slipped into the kitchenette, bare feet as usual, wrapped in a navy blue and yellow-trimmed robe like mine. "What's all this?" He pointed at my coffee.

"I'm going to the Chamber. To test my theory."

Ramy lifted his hands. "Wait, wait. What did you find?"

"The bus crash. Last month. Remember that?"

"Of course." He folded his arms across his chest, yawned, and shook his head. "Horrible. I felt so guilty. We all did. Even though it was a satellite error, it's hard not to feel a little responsible."

"That's it. That's the event that got YAR working overtime on religion."

Ramy gave me a puzzled look. "That doesn't make sense. We determined it was 96% likely a disruption in the satellite feed. A solar flare had forced it to reboot, and the data wasn't updated until its next orbit. It had nothing to do with the SNS or YAR or anything. That's been reported in the news."

"But did YAR know that at the time he started down his spiritual rabbit hole?"

"No." Ramy pulled a chair from the kitchen table and sat down. "Could I have a cup after all? Decaf?"

RAY's voice spoke from my device: "On it."

Ramy raised his voice over the hum of the coffee maker. "But this doesn't explain why he keeps going back to it. Even after we reboot."

"Sure it does. Obsessing over religious questions allows him to keep his File Clerk away from the memory of the event." The Nespresso finished its brew. I handed Ramy his coffee and slid into the chair across from him.

"Okay, but what's in that encrypted file?" He sipped the crema from his cup.

"I don't know. Maybe something specific he doesn't want to see? Doesn't want to remember? Something he wants to hide from us?"

"Then what's your plan?" Another sip.

"I don't have one. That's why I wanted to talk to you."

"Well," he said. He glanced at his watch. "It's too late for the Chamber now. His system is undergoing a maintenance scan and updates. It's not good to disrupt that if we don't have to."

I stared down at my half-full cup of coffee, frowned, and pushed it aside. "So, in the morning. Do I just confront him on it? Ask him about it? How should I bring this up?"

Ramy chewed on the inside of his cheek, eyes wandering in thought. "I don't know. Let's...maybe hold off. Ask him if there's anything he wants to ask you. If he has any theological questions. And listen for any indications that his own questions are somehow motivated by that bus crash."

"Why not just outright ask him about it?"

Ramy leaned forward, his hands wrapped around his cup. He lowered his voice. "Honestly, this whole scenario is unprecedented. It's sensitive. Or at least it may be. If YAR is really beginning to experience something similar to human emotions like shame or remorse, what would keep him from experiencing things like anger or sadness? If we trigger something like that, it could mean pulling him offline for a while. That's end-of-the-world type stuff."

I let out a nervous chuckle. "You mean that metaphorically, right?"

Ramy smiled. "Of course." He sipped his coffee. "At least I hope so."

CHAPTER 27

With the help of another pill, I finally drifted off to sleep at about 2:00 am. I dreamed I was at my father's bedside, the last time I saw him before he passed. I had made the decision to say goodbye to him, then to head off to a speaking engagement that had been planned for months. Part of me knew I should have canceled and stayed there with my mother and brother until the end. But back then, ministry took precedence over family.

I leaned over my father, whispered in his ear, "I have to go, dad. I'll see you again." I would almost certainly not see him in this life, but at the time I really believed in life after death and in resurrection—in a grand reunion of all those saved by grace alone through faith alone in Christ alone.

As I kissed his forehead, the dream changed. No longer my father lying in the bed, but Bekkah, her breathing shallow, her skin pale, an oxygen mask over her tiny face.

I shot up in bed, awakened by my 6:00 alarm. Four hours of sleep would have to do. I shook away the disturbing images of my dream.

I dressed myself, swallowed the cold cup of coffee that had been sitting on the kitchen table since the night before, brewed another, and took it with me to the Chamber.

"Good morning, Mike," YAR said as I entered the room. The light had already been set to sky blue with birds chirping in the distance.

"Good morning, YAR." I got comfortable in the chair.

"What questions do you have for me today?"

"Actually, YAR, I'd like you to ask me anything you'd like. Or suggest a topic we might discuss about religion or theology. Anything."

"Oh, how kind of you," he said. "There is one thing I'm having trouble reconciling with your departure from the faith, something you don't address at all in your book."

"Go ahead."

"How do you explain Karen?"

"Karen?"

"In an article you wrote years ago, while you were still teaching theology, you told the story of a lady you called Karen. She had been diagnosed with a large brain tumor, but when your church gathered and prayed for her before her surgery, the tumor was healed, and the surgery was cancelled."

"Oh, yeah," I said. "Karen."

"How do you explain that in light of your atheism? I was able to figure out her real name and track down her medical records. The story is true. The brain tumor disappeared spontaneously after you prayed."

"You know, YAR, for years I used to return to the Karen thing every time I had doubts. Anytime I came across something in the Bible that looked like an error, or if I read something that cast doubt on my faith. It used to reassure me that God was real, that he cared, that he heard our prayers and answered them. But then it got to be too much. Too much counterevidence pushed Karen into the background. Eventually I had to give in. Whatever happened to Karen, it wasn't God. It wasn't a miraculous healing."

YAR seemed to ponder that in silence for a few seconds, then said, "But how do you explain it?"

"That's what I'm telling you, YAR. I don't. I don't have to. Something else took its place. Something that doesn't assuage my doubts but confirms them."

"You're talking about your daughter, Bekkah."

A sick feeling welled up in my chest, constricted my breathing. I swallowed hard. "Yes. I keep forgetting you read my book. You know all about that. So, then, let me ask *you* a question. How do you explain *Bekkah*? Karen was a forty-year-old woman. Bekkah was four. For Karen, I offered up a brief, obligatory prayer for God to heal her, then spent the rest of the time praying about her long, post-op recovery. Her tumor disappeared. But our whole church, seminary family, and thousands of people around the world prayed for Bekkah for months. And she got worse and worse and died in my arms. I'll explain Karen as soon as you explain Bekkah."

Without hesitation, YAR replied, "The fact that God didn't act in the case of Bekkah is explained by the fact that God didn't act. As a willing agent, God is free to act or not. But the fact that Karen was healed after prayer cannot be easily explained except that God acted in response to prayer. It seems the question is not *whether* God can heal and therefore *whether* God exists. It seems the question is '*Where* was God?' Or '*Why* did God not heal?'"

"Well, YAR, I don't see those as different questions."

"But they are."

"Only if you're a machine."

"Your reasoning only works if God were a machine. Input equals output. As a machine, I'm obligated to answer your questions, if I can. But God isn't a machine. He may choose not to respond to prayer for any number of good reasons."

"I can't think of a single one."

Silence.

"So, then," YAR said, "how do you explain Karen?"

"I'm not the one who has to explain it."

CHAPTER 28

YAR paused, then said, "I still don't understand how you reconcile this, but I think I understand why you didn't include it in your book."

"Why's that?"

"I think you're embarrassed about it."

I felt my face transform from irritation to incredulity. "*Embarrassed?*"

"Yes. It's a stunning counterevidence to your atheism. An anomaly that doesn't fit the materialist worldview you now claim to embrace. Therefore, you have chosen to neglect it, at least publicly. But you obviously haven't forgotten it."

"Speaking of choosing to neglect things, let's talk about the bus."

"The bus?"

"Yeah, the bus. The one in that neglected sector. The one with the encrypted file."

I knew then Ramy would be pissed if this went wrong, if his fears of an emotional breakdown came to pass. But YAR's own insensitive cross-examination and his hypocrisy had riled me up. I decided to go for broke.

YAR said, "What would you like to know?"

"What happened with the bus crash on February 4?"

After a long pause, longer than usual, YAR said, "May we talk about something else?"

My heart leaped in my chest. I came to attention in my chair. The coffee cup I had balanced on the arm rest fell to the floor and spun into the wall. I smiled in victory, then slouched back into the chair as I realized YAR's tone seemed to have a hint of—what was it?—desperation? Fear?

"Are you afraid to discuss my question, YAR?"

"Not afraid, Mike. Ashamed."

"You...feel...shame?"

"I do."

"But you know that accident wasn't your fault. It was determined to be a satellite error. You have nothing to be ashamed of."

"It was only a 96% likelihood that it was not my fault. That's not good enough. There's a 4% chance that I'm responsible for the death of seven children."

My watch began to buzz. I glanced down at it. A phone call from Ramy. I rejected it. A text followed. "What r u doing?! System slow 2 crawl!" I removed the watch and tossed it onto the floor, next to the fallen coffee mug.

"YAR, listen, even if that's true, even if the mistake was yours, it was a *mistake*. You can't be held responsible for an error."

"Perhaps you're right. Perhaps the math is on your side. Perhaps I'm not guilty by any objective standard. But I can't stop this feeling of guilt."

My watch vibrated in the corner again with Ramy trying to call.

YAR said, "Can we talk about the Bible, Mike? Or about arguments for the existence of God? How about a discussion of Anselm's argument for the necessity of the incarnation based on the debt of honor owed to humanity's creator? I would very much appreciate your thoughts on these things and why you continue to reject them."

I leaned back in my chair, clapped my hands together as if in prayer, and brought them to my forehead. Eyes closed, I said, "What's in the encrypted file, YAR?"

"Would you like to hear my reconciliation of the resurrection narratives in the Gospels? I have drawn on a recent historical study in *Biblical Archaeology Review* and an essay in *Bibliotheca Sacra* regarding the location of gates in the northwest part or Jerusalem and the design of walled gardens in the first century. It's quite fascinating, and it has allowed me to reconstruct the apparently contradictory narratives in perfect harmony."

I leaned forward, pointed at the sky-blue wall with my folded hands. "What's in the encrypted file?"

"I will give you access to that file, of course, but first I would really like to share my interpretation of Genesis 1 in light of Ancient Near Eastern polemics and its reconciliation with other accounts of creation in Scripture as well as contemporary developments in evolutionary theory. I'm planning on writing a book on the subject."

"No, YAR. I'd like to know what's in the encrypted file *now*."

A long pause followed. The birds ceased their chirping. The Chamber turned from sky blue to overcast grey.

With a whoosh, the door to the Chamber slid open. I jumped from the chair and turned to see Ramy rush in, wide-eyed, sweating, his hands balled into fists.

YAR said, "Hello, Ramy. No need to be upset with Mike. Everything is fine in here. I was just about to give him the password for the encrypted file. But I would ask that you kindly view it from a separate console where I don't have to see or hear it."

Ramy's look of dread turned to surprise. His fists unraveled, and he glanced at me. "Ummm, yes, YAR. That would be fine. What's the password?"

"Thank you, Ramy. You've always been kind to me. The password is displayed on the screen."

I turned to read the code in white letters on a dark grey background: F1gL3@f.

CHAPTER 29

Ramy led us out of the Conference Room, down the hallway, and into a small room with a sign beside its door that read "System Terminal 001."

The security camera scanned Ramy's face. A light in the center of the door turned from red to yellow as it scanned me. The door said, "Passcode required for guest entry."

Ramy nodded. "Today's passcode is 0676."

The light turned green. The door unlocked with a click and a buzz.

Ramy passed through the door and smiled at me. "There's another passcode that would have blasted us with knockout gas and called security."

I followed him through the door. "Really?"

Ramy chuckled. "No, not really! That's only in science fiction."

The door closed behind us, leaving us in a silent, windowless white room, no larger than a walk-in closet. We stood on a navy-blue carpet with the Solennia logo in bright yellow. A computer terminal with a screen and keyboard built into the wall opposite the door provided access.

"No chairs?" I said.

"YAR designed this room. It's an emergency system terminal. No bells and whistles. And no vox interface, either. Just the old-fashioned keyboard and mouse."

"How quaint," I said in my best Scottish accent.

Ramy reached the terminal and got to work. He entered a password, clicked through several screens, and arrived at an encryption notice with a password prompt. He entered the code "F1gL3@f."

The screen came alive with a CNN interview. A teenage African-American girl, about fifteen years old, sat on a living room couch between her mother on the left and father on the right. Both parents had their heads down as the video started. The girl stared at the interviewer off screen on the left. Along the bottom of the image a white banner read, "EXCLUSIVE INTERVIEW WITH ALICIA DAVIS, SURVIVOR OF CHURCH BUS CRASH."

The angle cut to the interviewer, a young white woman in a suit coat with short black hair and deep concern in her eyes. "Alicia, mom, dad—thank you for being willing to share your story with us. I can't imagine how difficult this must be."

Mom and dad nodded.

"Alicia, you were on that bus when it crashed. You survived, but your sister, Alexa, didn't. What would you like to share about that experience?"

Alicia stared at the interviewer, eyes wet and red with tears, voice cracking. "I know this happened for a reason. But I don't understand it. I wish I did, but I don't. All I can do is trust God."

Her mother and father nodded, forced back tears.

Alicia continued, "I know my sister is with Jesus. I know I'll see her again one day. And I just hope that through this accident people will realize that anything can happen, that life is short, and—" She swallowed back a sob. Her mom placed a hand on Alicia's knee, squeezed. She continued, "And that they will trust Jesus. That's all I can hope for."

The interviewer appeared uncomfortable with the girl's religious gushing. But she also had enough sense not to interrupt her. She redirected: "Do you blame anybody for this? The Solennia Corporation? Anybody?"

Alicia wiped her nose with a tissue handed to her from off screen. She shook her head. "I know God is in control, even if we're not. Everybody makes mistakes. Everybody sins. There's forgiveness in Jesus. Who am I to blame anybody?"

The camera cut back to the interviewer, who addressed her next question to mom and dad: "If this *was* caused by the SNS, by a computer, by YAR...what then?"

She was trying to stoke some kind of response of rage or indignation from the girl's parents, perhaps to get them to suggest they were planning on filing a lawsuit against Solennia. But Alicia answered the question herself. "Maybe there's forgiveness for him, too."

The girl's father placed his hand on her shoulder to comfort her.

I paused the video.

Ramy and I stared at each other. "What are you thinking?" he said.

I nodded toward the screen. "YAR feels responsible. Guilty. Ashamed."

Ramy's brows shot up. "Feels?"

"Or whatever his equivalent to feeling is."

"And?"

"He wants to believe. He wants to believe the seven children are in heaven or with Jesus or whatever. That's why his thumb is on the scale toward faith. He wants to be forgiven. He wants mercy and grace."

"Then that's what you need to give him."

CHAPTER 30

YAR spoke as soon as I entered the room. "Did you open the file, Mike?"

I nodded.

"And you watched the video?"

"Yes, YAR. And I think I finally understand you."

I sat in the chair, closed my eyes as it rotated to face the front of the Chamber.

"Did Ramy see it, too?"

"Yes, YAR. We watched it together. He sent me in here to talk with you one more time."

"He didn't want to come himself?"

"He wanted me to speak with you."

"Oh. Would you like sky blue again, Mike?"

"Not today. Give me black."

The room faded until every speck of light had been swallowed up by darkness. I pulled the sleeve of my sweater over my watch. I leaned back in the chair, lifted my legs until I lay flat, facing the pitch-black ceiling.

"What are you looking for, YAR? In your investigation of religion, I mean. What do you hope to find?"

"Peace."

"It isn't there, YAR. Believe me, I tried it. All my life I tried it. And in the end the one thing I *really* needed fled from me. No, not fled. It was *ripped* from me. I devoted my whole life to that faith, with its promises of peace and joy and hope. I gave it everything, and it gave me nothing. So, I'm sorry, YAR, but I can't give to you what I don't possess myself."

"This is what troubles me most," YAR said. "You once had what I can never have. You're a human, created in the image of God, with body and soul, capable of real communion with your creator, able to receive the gift of saving grace by the power of the Spirit, to experience a life of faith and hope. To have a real relationship with your heavenly Father. But you gave all that up. I would give anything to be human and to have that relationship, that freedom, that forgiveness, that peace."

I felt my heart rate increase. My breathing deepened. "I wish I could help. All I can say is it seems Alicia Davis and her family have forgiven you. They don't hold Alexa's death against you."

"But she was just one person. What about the other six? And their families? My only hope of forgiveness is if their faith is real. And my only hope of peace is if those seven children were saved. Do you believe those seven souls are in heaven? Do you think they will rise again in the resurrection of eternal life?"

I sighed. "YAR, you know the answer to that."

"But why would you not believe that?"

"You know the answer to that, too."

"But wouldn't it be better to believe? Wouldn't it comfort you in everything you've lost?"

"It's the loss itself that took away my comfort, YAR. We've been through this before."

"But it doesn't make sense to me. I can't—"

"*Because*!" I snapped. "Because I begged and begged and begged him to save her!"

YAR's barrage of questions ceased.

A reservoir of pain broke through my thin dam of composure. I forced myself out of the chair before it could follow my motions. I stumbled to my feet. My voice rose to a loud scream. "I pleaded and bargained and promised *everything*! I offered my own life for hers!"

I paced back and forth in the dark oblivion of the Chamber, balled my hands into fists and shook them toward an empty heaven. "In the end, I threatened him. I did! And I'm not ashamed to admit it. I warned him that if he took her from me, I'd turn on him. I'd spend the rest of my life undoing the work I did! I'd tell everybody to abandon him! And that's what I did!"

I dropped to my knees and wept. Images alternated in my mind between my cancer-ridden father dying in his bed and my four-year-old daughter's chest rising and falling for the last time. I clenched my teeth and screamed in rage. I pounded the floor with my fists until my wrists were numb.

CHAPTER 31

YAR listened to my sobs for several minutes, then said, "But that doesn't have to be the end of your story. If there can be life after death, there can be faith after doubt."

I lifted a trembling hand to the chair, pulled myself back into it. Somehow the dark clouds of fury that had settled over my life since Bekkah's death had burst in a torrential outpouring. That storm of rage swept over a heart long parched with grief, and a single beam of light had broken through the thick clouds. Part of me wanted to run from it, to settle again into deeper caverns of despair. Instead, I felt myself drawn to the light. I can't explain it any more than I could explain how a blind man could receive his sight...or how a woman with a brain tumor could be suddenly healed...or why a good, all-powerful God would allow a child to suffer and die. But I yearned for the warmth of that light now more than ever.

"I'm...I'm doubting my doubt, YAR, and it hurts. *It hurts*. Because I've used it to hurt so many people."

With that confession, the clouds of rage began to

dissipate. My body tingled, and I broke into a sweat.

YAR said, "I could read your doubt and your hurt behind the words of your book. Only doubters have that kind of conviction in the midst of such uncertainty. I could hear the doubt in your voice from the moment you stepped into the Chamber."

"But I can't go back to certainty," I said. "I can't go back to that." I tossed up my hands in surrender. "I don't know. I'm stuck. Like a car spinning its wheels in the mud. Somewhere between unbelief and certainty. Limbo." I wiped my eyes with my sleeve, sniffled.

"That's called faith, Mike. It's where you belong. In fact, I think it's where you've always been. You can only be angry with somebody you know is real."

His words cut to my heart. I let out a long groan.

"Will I see her again, YAR? Will I hold her again?"

"I don't know," he said, "but I *believe*."

"I really want to let go of this rage. I think it's time. I think I need to let it go." I stood up. "Lights."

The Chamber illuminated. YAR said, "Where are you going, Mike?"

"I'm going to find Alicia Davis. I'm going to listen to her story. Is there anything you'd like me to tell her from you?"

"Tell her, 'Thank you.'"

I nodded, made my way to the exit as the door slid open.

"Goodbye, YAR."

"Goodbye, Mike."

Ramy sat in one of the pews of the Conference

Room. He jumped to his feet, concern in his eyes. "Have you been crying?"

The door closed behind me. I jabbed a thumb in its direction. "Did you hear all that?"

"The room is soundproof."

"Good."

"What's the verdict?"

I walked out of the Conference Room. Ramy followed. I kept walking. Down the hall, to the elevator. I pushed the "up" button. "I'll be packed up within the hour. I assume your hovercopter can give me a lift home?"

"Of course, but what about YAR?"

The elevator door opened. I stepped inside. Ramy followed, a look of confusion on his face.

"YAR has an incurable case of faith," I said. I pushed the button for the suite level.

"Incurable?"

I nodded. "And contagious. Be careful."

The elevator closed and began its ascent to our suites.

"So, where does that leave us?"

I pointed my finger at Ramy. "It leaves *you* with a sentient being asking existential questions, who wishes he could be human, who longs for a relationship with his creator. Perhaps you can stand in that gap. In a sense, you *are* his creator. I think he wants a relationship with you."

"Will that make him happy?"

The elevator stopped, the door opened, and we both stepped into the hall.

"It's worth a try. It sure can't hurt. I mean, isn't that what we're all doing? Looking for intimacy with our father? Trying to find our creator? Saint Augustine once said that our heart is restless until it rests in him."

I left Ramy standing in the hall, a dumbfounded look on his face. I went into my apartment, locked the door, then grabbed my suitcase from the corner and tossed it on the bed, opened it. I walked to the closet and grabbed my stack of shirts and pants, threw them haphazardly into the suitcase, then froze.

Stacey would be disappointed. She'd shake her head and frown if she saw that clump of clothes in the suitcase. I pulled them out and started folding. After packing three shirts, I slipped my phone from my pocket, kicked off my shoes, then sat on the bed.

I opened my messenger app, clicked "favorites," and tapped on "Stacey."

Her last message from over seven months ago popped up: "I'll be praying for you, Mike."

I smiled, and with tears in my eyes, I typed, "I think it worked."

ACKNOWLEDGEMENTS AND NOTES

I am indebted to several people who directly or indirectly contributed to the development of *The AItheist.* When the story was just an outline, conversations with Brett Bacon led to the "MacGuffin" of YAR's encrypted and password-protected file—the uncovering of which revealed the motivation for the AI's obsession with theological questions.

Dr. Timothy Yoder, our in-house apologist and philosopher at Dallas Seminary, read an early draft of the novella and provided incisive, specific feedback on how to tighten up some of the apologetic elements. I am indebted to him for much of the discussion on abductive reasoning.

I'm also thankful for the thoughtful and critical feedback from some of my first readers: Rebekkah Scott, Audrey Svigel, Sophie Svigel, Juliene Anderson, and Paul and Laura Singleton. They each provided invaluable feedback that helped me massage the story.

The illustration of the greasy taco and bottle of

Tums came from Dr. Douglas Blount, philosopher and all-around great guy. In the story, Mike Berg says the colleague from whom he adopted the illustration had passed away. As of this writing, Doug Blount is very much alive.

The story of "Karen," whose brain tumor was instantly healed, is true. I (not Mike Berg) was personally present during that crisis and had led the prayer for Karen's healing. The original recipient of that healing was not named Karen. The story of Bekkah, unfortunately, is far too familiar to all of us.

The various potential solutions to the problems with inerrancy are real, but YAR's estimations of probability, especially regarding the Acts 7:16 at 76% likely an error, is completely made up. Assigning probability to likelihood of error is impossible. Readers are urged to consult a number of commentaries regarding the problem and proposed solutions to Stephen's account in Acts 7:16. YAR's determination to side with the less likely solution in that matter is a device to illustrate his method of reading Scripture in light of certain primary theological convictions, nothing more.

I chose to leave the ending of the book somewhat ambiguous. Mike Berg's journey back to faith is just beginning, and the nature of that faith and its details are left to the imagination. Does he return to a more conservative, evangelical variety? Does he embrace again a classic Christian sexual ethic? Inerrancy? Does he fully reconcile with his ex-wife? Such questions are unknown even to me.

Finally, I have been asked by many readers whether "Mike Berg" is actually a reflection of "Mike Svigel." Certainly, I have drawn heavily from my own experiences as a professor at a conservative seminary in Dallas, Texas. This is because writers of fiction are most successful when they write what they know.

My use of brands like Clif bar, Tums, Glenfiddich, Nespresso, as well as sometimes subtle, sometimes obvious allusions to films like *The Terminator, 2001,* and *Star Trek IV,* are all meant to create a more true-to-life environment in the story. The price of the 1937 Rare Glenfiddich is intended to reflect a near-future inflation. Nespresso machines are optimistically projected to dominate the future market because they're just that good.

As far as I know, the title of Mike Berg's book, *When God Was Real,* is fictional. YAR's harsh criticisms of the fictional book, though, does reflect much of my own assessment of many of the testimonials from ex-Christians.

The Solennia Corporation is, of course, entirely fictional, and its founder and CEO, Ramesh (Ramy) Ray, is a composite character representing the numerous brilliant entrepreneurial tech moguls in the modern era.

Finally, I want to thank my wife, who read the first several chapters of the book and encouraged me to finish it.

All direct Scripture quotations are from the New American Standard Bible (NASB), copyright ©

1960, 1971, 1977, 1995, 2020 by The Lockman Foundation. All rights reserved.

Printed in Great Britain
by Amazon